The Lord's Taverners
CRICKET CLINIC
TACTICS • TECHNIQUES • TRAINING

The Lord's Taverners
CRICKET CLINIC
TACTICS • TECHNIQUES • TRAINING

with

Trevor Bailey · Alec Bedser · Richie Benaud · Dickie Bird
Mike Brearley · Colin Cowdrey · Ted Dexter · Mike Gatting
Alf Gover · Jim Laker · John Lever · Peter May · Bill O'Reilly
Derek Randall · Viv Richards · Bobby Simpson · Bob Taylor
Bernard Thomas · Fred Trueman · Derek Underwood

Coaching instructions : Alf Gover

A Graham Tarrant Book

David & Charles
Newton Abbot   London   North Pomfret (Vt)

Other Contributors	
Biographical notes	**David Foot**
Photography (unless otherwise stated)	**Ken Kelly**
Coaching illustrations	**Rodger Towers**
Design	**Michael Head**

British Library Cataloguing in Publication Data

The Lord's Taverners cricket clinic. –
  (A Graham Tarrant book)
  1. Cricket
  796.35'82   GV917

  ISBN 0-7153-8777-4

The Lord's Taverners and the Publishers are grateful to
the following for permission to use material from works
in copyright:
Hodder & Stoughton for *The Art of Captaincy* by Mike
Brearley; Lutterworth Press for *Alf Gover's Cricket
Manual* (including source material for some of the
coaching illustrations); Derek Randall for *The Young
Player's Guide to Cricket* (written with Terry Bowles).

© The Lord's Taverners 1986

Typeset by Typesetters (Birmingham) Ltd
Smethwick   West Midlands
and printed in Great Britain
by Butler & Tanner Ltd   Frome and London
for David & Charles Publishers plc
Brunel House   Newton Abbot   Devon

Published in the United States of America
by David & Charles Inc
North Pomfret   Vermont 05053   USA

*Cover photograph: A panoramic view of Old
Trafford taken during the England v Australia Test
match in 1985* (Ken Kelly)

CONTENTS

A WORD ABOUT
THE LORD'S TAVERNERS

Cricket has been our business since we became a registered charity in 1950. The Lord's Taverners give grant-aid for coaching, competitions, cricket equipment and artificial pitches for all clubs who run Colts sides. With the demise of cricket in schools, particularly in the state sector, it has become increasingly important to help clubs who wish to encourage young people to play the noblest of summer games.

All our money is channelled through the National Cricket Association, the governing body of cricket outside the first-class game. They, in turn, co-ordinate bids from the forty-eight County Associations throughout the country. Each year we grant-aid, in some shape or form, 400 clubs. The other beneficiary is the English Schools Cricket Association who are affiliated to the NCA and have a special responsibility for schoolboys.

In conjunction with ESCA and *The Cricketer* magazine, The Lord's Taverners sponsor each year the largest cricket competition in the world for some 1500 schools. The final is always held on a Test match ground.

Coaching the nursery game is, therefore, one of our primary charitable objectives. To this end *Cricket Clinic* is dedicated.

Our thanks to the many famous Lord's Taverners and others who have pooled their resources and skills in this unique book on coaching. Whilst there have been many books on this subject, *Cricket Clinic* presents to young players and coaches alike the collective views of a team of experts which is unsurpassed.

Anthony Swainson OBE
Director

HOOKING, PULLING & SWEEPING: VIV RICHARDS

Viv Richards

Many, including chastened and savaged bowlers, have cited him as the best batsman in the world over the past ten years or so. He has been inclined to trifle with their faith by rushes of blood and other aberrations. At times he has looked almost too weary to lift the bat. Blame the relentless schedule of his cricketing diary and not the man.

He has all the shots, most of them classically based. He prefers fours and sixes to singles. He prefers adventure to futile occupation of the crease. At times he strikes the ball dangerously because he believes the element of danger – and fallibility – are part of the appeal of cricket. He started, home in Antigua, as an off-side player. His cover-drive is often in the Hammond class, so exquisite is the timing and effortless power.

But he taught himself to use the leg side more. He saw nothing seriously wrong with a minor liberty or two over line if the feet were right. Nowadays he veers from orthodoxy with a languid smile on his handsome face, as the ball rockets through mid-wicket. The hooks and the pulls can be murderous. He scored 322 against Warwickshire on a searingly hot day at Taunton in 1985 and his first compliment went to Gladstone Small, who bowled so well with such little success.

Viv Richards made his debut for Leeward Islands in 1971–2 and for Somerset, after a year's qualification playing mostly club cricket in Bath, in 1974. He was an instant success and was selected for the West Indian tour of India in 1974–5. Since then the centuries, for country and county, have soared. One of his great ambitions was fulfilled when he was made captain of West Indies, in succession to his mentor, Clive Lloyd.

He has been used increasingly by Somerset as an extra bowler, switching from off-break to gentle seam according to the state of the pitch (or the match). His fielding, whether in the slips, covers or the boundary edge in the one-day matches, is exemplary. He has a long memory and the suggestion of a short fuse. He's a loyal friend and team-mate. To see Richards and Botham, side by side and at their outrageous best, offers a privileged and imperishable memory for West Country spectators.

Viv Richards hitting to leg during his innings of 232 against England at Trent Bridge in 1976. The great West Indian's lightning reflexes and dazzling footwork enable him to get into position very early to play his shots.

Hooking, Pulling & Sweeping

I started out very much as an off-side player. Back in my schooldays I was always proud of my cover drive. Everyone told me it was the best shot in the book. So what am I doing now, telling you how I play the hook, the pull and the sweep?

Well, of course, it's a fact that many of my runs these days come from the leg side. That has been the result of a very deliberate effort on my part to extend the repertoire of my shots. It first occurred to me as a teenager that I should develop my on-side play. A batsman happy to limit his scoring strokes to one side of the wicket – the one that comes naturally to him – is always going to be at a disadvantage.

The shots I am about to discuss all have an element of danger with them. There are pitfalls – as I know to my cost. But the last thing I would want to do is discourage a batsman from walking to the wicket with a sense of adventure. It's a large

Perfectly balanced as he goes down on one knee, Alvin Kallicharran sweeps a ball from Derek Underwood to the boundary. Wicket-keeper Alan Knott appears to have been seized with stomach cramp.

part of the appeal of cricket and I hope I can succeed in persuading you not to fight shy of it.

The secret is to be fully aware of the dangers. That way, you can minimise the risks. I can't emphasise too much that we are talking about a game played with the *mind* as well as the body. The opposition will be trying all the time to outwit you, to 'psyche' you out and tempt you to make the kind of mistake you'll regret so bitterly on the long walk back to the pavilion.

Now let's start with the hook. There have been times in my career when I've been a compulsive hooker. It's a great source of runs, of course. The ball is short-pitched and maybe a thoroughly bad one – so, one argues impulsively, it has to be carted into the crowd.

But wait a minute. Was it a bad ball or one deliberately schemed by the bowler? You must have recalled how often Ian Botham was criticised for those short-pitched deliveries of his in the recent series with Australia. Yet pause to accept how often they brought him success. Players like Andrew Hilditch made a dreadful mess of their intended hooks and only gave a straightforward catch.

As a bowler, Ian Botham is far more of a theorist

than people realise. Someone one day will work out just how many wickets he has taken from deliveries that were deliberately dropped short to entice an unwise and unwary batsman to hook into the waiting arms of a leg-side fielder.

People are apt to ask me the best hooker I have seen. I have no difficulty answering that. I nominate Roy Fredericks, the little, beautifully co-ordinated Guyanese batsman. His timing was perfect. His feet were always right. And, almost as important, he knew where the fielders were placed. He never gave his wicket away irresponsibly when he went to hook.

Bowlers aren't all as cunning as Botham. Many haven't got the sheer confidence to keep digging the ball in short and risking punishment. Some learn the hard way.

We had a likeable bowler called Uton George Dowe, a Jamaican, who played in four Tests for us and took 12 wickets from them. He was well built, had a long run-up and an aggressive appearance as he approached the wicket. He was also apt to be pretty wild.

Keith Stackpole was an Australian batsman with a reputation for being very strong on the hook shot. He was a fine back-foot player, like so many of the Aussies, and though he was inclined to be lucky when it came to chances in the slips, he was pretty powerful and ruthless when there was an opportunity to hook. I've heard the story many times of how my fellow countrymen warned Dowe. 'Keep the ball up to him.'

The Jamaican fast bowler decided he would find out for himself, the hard way. In five overs or so, poor old Dowe was savaged. He kept digging them in short – and Stackpole, always a favourite with the spectators in any case, kept whacking for six.

I come back to Roy Fredericks. On my very first tour of Australia in 1975–6, the memories weren't all ones to cherish. We only came out on top in one Test, for a start. Losing the series 5–1 isn't too good for the morale. But what I shall always remember of that tour was a wonderful knock of 169 by Fredericks in the Perth Test. He just kept on hooking the fast bowlers.

Everything that is right about the daring hook shot was there on view. He was completely unconcerned about the pace of the wicket. He made the fielders redundant.

The hook is exciting – and, as I've said,

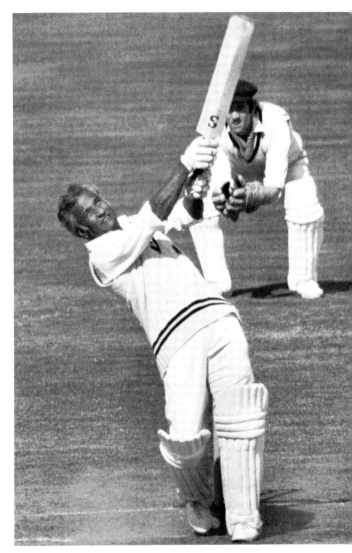

Playing for Warwickshire against Derbyshire in 1972, West Indian Rohan Kanhai pulls a ball from England fast bowler Alan Ward into the crowd for a towering six.

dangerous. Some great cricketers never bothered with it at all. Their natures, it seems to me, were just a little too cautious. And that was rather a pity. Let me try to advise when . . . and how.

Most of us, as batsmen, have got a weakness. It doesn't take long for it to get known on the county grapevine. It's the same among the local clubs. There is a surprising number of batsmen who can't resist giving their wickets away with a miscalculated hook.

Even the mighty fall for an old trick once in a while. Viv Richards hooks a short ball from Ian Botham straight into the hands of Paul Allott at long leg, giving his Somerset team-mate his 299th Test wicket.

I'm going to take the hook, the pull and the sweep in rotation. Let's assume you have the ability – or at least the enthusiasm – to try them.

First, THE HOOK. This is for the ball that has been pitched short and is coming at waist height or perhaps higher than that. Maybe it's a rank bad ball and deserves to go. Maybe it's a high-risk delivery. So, if I can mix my metaphors and take a phrase from another favourite sport of mine, boxing, don't fall for the sucker punch.

Unless you are supremely confident, you shouldn't start hooking as soon as you get to the crease in any case. Take a long, hard look at the bowling (I'm not talking about limited-overs cricket when the need for runs takes over from caution!). Take an even longer and harder look at the field placings. Tell yourself, as you see those lurking leg-side fielders, that you aren't going to fall for that one.

When schoolboys back in Antigua or at Taunton ask me how they should hook, I begin by telling them that they must get into position very quickly indeed. There's no time for indecision. Once they're in position, I say, they are still able to change their mind. If the ball comes rearing up, full of menace and is difficult to reach, then leave it. Let it go over your shoulder, I tell them. Perhaps it won't come at sufficient height to allow a hook.

If it's there to be hit, do it in the proper way. The right foot (for the right-hander) goes back and across the stumps, inside the line of flight. One of the difficulties is making sure you can get on top of the ball, rolling the wrists to make sure that the ball doesn't soar into the air. It's all controlled.

Yes, I know all about the thrilling sight of fast bowlers being fearlessly hooked for six, high into the crowd at square and long leg. But you need to be very sure of yourself – and probably lucky, too – to get away with it. The best hook shots are those that are kept low and still elude the fielders. So the wrist is important. So is your sense of balance. And so is your judgment – being able to decide whether to go for the hook or leave well alone. The hook calls for a neat pivot movement, and you can't have too much practice.

THE PULL. It doesn't look so good. Sports masters (as I remember from my own days back in St John's) shake their heads. They just aren't happy about one of their promising pupils taking a ball outside the off stump and hammering it away through the leg side.

Why ever not? Provided you get to the pitch of the ball and remain fully in control, there is nothing ugly and unwise about the pull.

So, there are a few basic rules to observe. The pull shot is played to the short ball from the slow or medium-paced bowler – or to the full toss. The bowler has probably strayed accidentally in his length and deserves to concede some runs.

That juicy long-hop, first. Move your back foot across and make sure your head is behind the ball. Your feet should be apart to guarantee good balance. As for the full toss, no-one at the crease likes to let the bowler get away with that. Get your weight on the front foot as it eases towards the ball. Make contact with your arms at full stretch. Roll the wrists to avoid putting the ball in the air for a simple catch. And, like most of my West Indian mates, I do like to see a generous follow-through. That means for the pull as well as other more rhythmic shots.

Now THE SWEEP. I've never really favoured the shot myself. But that shouldn't imply it's to be avoided. Again the advice is fundamental – *play it correctly and you won't go wrong.*

I used to watch clips of Mike Smith on the telly. He played the sweep so well. In my case, it used to become my downfall and I worked hard to improve it. After all, it's a very useful way of scoring against the ball pitched well up, outside the leg stump. The whole thing is a *sweeping motion.*

The rules? Get the left (or forward) foot inside the line of the ball. That helps you to protect your stumps. Now 'sweep' – it doesn't need to be a very physical effort. All you are really doing is helping the ball on its way.

Finally, just a word about my so-called CLIP through mid-wicket. It's the one I take off a delivery aimed at or even outside my off stump. Tut-tut! Yes, I know it breaks a few rules and the purists are inclined to disapprove. But it brings me generous runs and, if the timing is right, can look attractive.

My closing words – about the clip and the various other shots I've tried to describe – are this. Get to the pitch of the ball and your troubles are virtually over. If the hook, pull or sweep, however, continue to bring you problems, be sensible enough to avoid them. There's a difference between the sense of adventure I advocate . . . and sheer folly.

Ian Botham hitting New Zealand's Lance Cairns for six at Trent Bridge in 1983. (Left) Botham pivots on his right foot to hook the ball high into the stand, backward of square. (Right) The momentum of the shot has him finishing with his left foot wide of the off stump, his arms fully extended behind him.

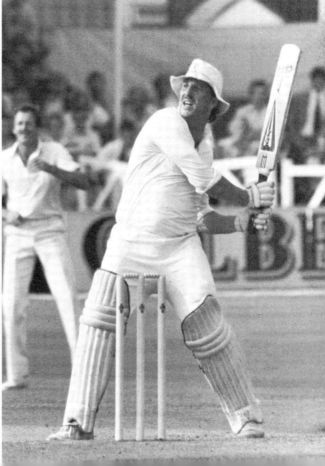

Hook

Played to the very short, fast delivery coming down in a line towards the middle or leg stump and arriving at chest height or above.

1 The bat goes high with the wrists dropping back and the right foot well across to take the head and upper part of the body away from the line of the oncoming ball.

2 Back view. The left foot comes off the ground, helping the pivot of the shoulders sideways on. The right elbow close to the side. The right wrist fully cocked.

3 The hit is made. The hands are high. The head and shoulders are still out of the 'line of fire'. The right hand puts the power in the shot. The left arm is bent and high. The eyes follow the ball on to the bat.

4 The bat follows through in a complete arc around the left side. The right elbow has come up as the right hand turned over to put the power into the shot. The body balance rocks back with the bat's follow-through. The head is steady, the eyes watching the result of the shot.

Pull

Played to the short-of-a-length ball from the slow or medium-paced bowler, pitching on or around the off stump.

1 The right foot goes back well outside the off stump. The bat is lifted to the high pick-up position. The left shoulder faces the oncoming ball. The right foot points in the direction of extra cover. The balance of the body is on the right leg.

2 The hit is about to be made. The arms go away from the body. The shoulders come square on with the swing of the bat. The right wrist is cocked. The right foot points up the wicket with the shoulder movement.

3 The hit is made, the right wrist turning the face of the bat over to play the ball down. The right hand powers the shot, the left arm maintains the swing of the bat. The eyes watch the ball all the way.

4 There is a full pivot as the right hand, having pulled the ball round from off to leg, continues its momentum around the body.

Sweep

Played to the ball pitching short of the half-volley on or outside the leg stump. It can be used against either the off-spinner, hitting *with* the turn, or the leg-spinner, hitting *against* the turn.

1 The left foot goes out inside the line of the ball. Both knees are bent, allowing the balance to occur over the haunches. The shoulders begin to open slightly. Both wrists are fully cocked. The hands are dropping the bat in order to flatten the arc of the cross swing at the ball.

2 The arc of the bat has been flattened. The wrists are still bent. The left arm controls the swing of the bat. Both arms are slightly bent.

3 The hit is made. The right wrist is uncocked as the right hand punches the ball away. The balance is maintained. The head is steady, the body pivots at the hips.

4 The complete follow-through. The trunk has completed almost a full turn, but the body balance is still constant on the haunches. The left arm bends, allowing the swing of the right hand and arm to finish its impetus.

CUTTING: TED DEXTER

Ted Dexter

'Lord Ted': ah well, now we're getting to the aristocracy. It's a fact of the human condition that not all blue bloods are loved. Ted Dexter didn't arguably top every popularity poll but everyone admired his style. That, on a cricket field, meant a pathological inclination to launch an assault on the bowlers – the pace merchants as well as the spinners. He was prepared to lay into Hall and Griffith, and not many dared to do that.

One remembers him not just for the dash and relish of his driving. The aficionados always approved of the minimum of movement as he stood, braced for action, at the crease. His stillness was similar to that of Viv Richards. Above all, he looked good. He was a handsome figure – and collected his runs, from choice, with handsome rapidity. Not that he couldn't defend with unwavering correctness. It was just that he was happiest in the role of cavalier.

He *had* to be captain. That was what he was at Radley, Cambridge, Sussex and inevitably England. Possibly he wasn't made to take orders from someone else. It was argued that his heart was never wholly in cricket and that could be a fair assumption. Yet he scored more than 21,000 first-class runs and took 419 wickets. He made 62 Test appearances. These are impressive statistics, especially when we remember that his career was interrupted when he broke a leg in 1965. Back he came, persuaded by his chums, three years later. He immediately hit a double century against Kent and there were optimistic hopes around Hove that his Test career could be relaunched. He did, in fact, make two more appearances for England: then he moved over to his typewriter on Saturdays.

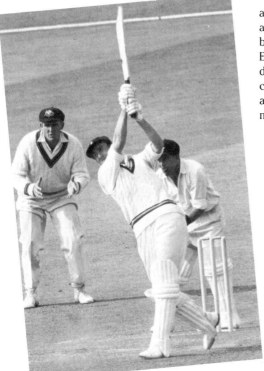

An England captain who goes for his shots must always be something of a national hero. Ted Dexter's aggressive courage against the West Indians will long be savoured. So will those mighty innings of his, at Edgbaston and Old Trafford in 1961 and 1964, when he demonstrated with marvellous defiance that matches could be saved against the Australians. He was indeed an adaptable player. That was why he had no trouble mixing his cricket with his golf swing.

Ted Dexter hitting out during his great match-saving innings of 180 for England against Australia at Edgbaston in 1961. In all, he batted for 344 minutes and hit 31 fours. Also in the picture are Alan Davidson and wicket-keeper Wally Grout.

A typically spectacular square cut from Gordon Greenidge, playing for West Indies against England at The Oval in 1976. Perfect balance and timing, coupled with immense power, sends the ball crashing to the boundary.

Cutting

There are more runs to be scored off the back foot than the front. The range of shots is greater and so it's an obvious advantage if you are the kind of batsman who can get runs off the shorter ball.

During my career I particularly relished the straight drive and it was a valuable source of runs. But front-foot play tends to be directed to a relatively restricted arc. It's different as a back player – and that means for the square and the late cut, as well as the hook.

Let me start with a golden rule. *Don't try to cut the ball coming into you.* Certainly until you are very well set indeed, you must never for a moment consider cutting the off-spinner or the inswinger.

Australian Doug Walters plays his own version of the square cut to a short ball outside the off stump. Relying more on timing and placement than on power, he uses his wrists to whip the ball away square of the wicket.

If the ball starts coming back into you the danger is that you will tend to nick and give a catch.

The cut *needs to be used with caution.* However experienced the batsman, the cut demands expert timing. It's so fraught with perils. Too often, the intended cut can end with a catch to the wicket-keeper or the slips – maybe to cover or a top edge to third man.

The batsman needs to know the bounce of the ball before he starts cutting. Pace of the wicket is also important. But let me come to the essentials, if you aim to be a good cutter. The bat *must be picked up high enough* in the first place. There are two points to remember here – make sure the hands are sufficiently high up the handle, and that the oil-hole end of the bat is aiming for the sky. Just take a look at David Gower or Ian Botham the next time their batting is being televised.

What happens from that position is that you are coming right down on the ball and not simply glancing it. Ideally the face of the bat – when at its highest point – should be pointing at the cover boundary and not towards the ground. You are then perfectly placed for the blade to crack down on the ball.

The good cutters remember these basics. Those who get themselves out from the cut too often restrict their back-lift, or have the bat 'shut' (as we say), facing to the ground.

We'll start with the SQUARE CUT. It can be played to either the slow or fast bowler but you will have more time and tend to square-cut the slow bowler more frequently. You need to be looking for the delivery which is perhaps eighteen inches wide of the stumps – and *you need room to play the shot.* Be wary of the one that is 'too close for comfort'. We've all seen players running into problems, getting 'tucked-up' as it's known, because they haven't been able to make enough room for themselves.

The ball must have reasonable bounce so that you can control it. If it stays down, you could be in trouble and drag on, off the inside edge.

As a general rule, I'd never recommend the square cut off the front foot. To me, it's a bit of a fancy stroke, only played as you move your foot forward to a shortish ball when really you should have gone back. On very flat wickets you might get a forward player appearing to cut the ball square but then more accurately it's a square drive.

Now I come to the LATE CUT. This is, in effect,

just a refinement of *placing the ball.* You let it come a little further past you and simply use the pace of the ball to direct it between slips and gully.

Cutting, especially the late cut, comes more easily to you and you play it far better if the body is *sideways to the line.* This allows you to let the ball come beside and past you before you play the shot. If you are square-on, it's increasingly difficult to play the ball late.

I liked cutting myself. I got into the right

Rolling the wrists in textbook fashion, Basil D'Oliveira executes the perfect late cut off a ball from the Pakistan leg-spinner Intikhab Alam. Wicket-keeper Wasim Bari looks on.

position to do it and I had the advantage of a fairly generous backlift. And I'd like to encourage you to bring it more and more into your repertoire, remembering the basic rules and the pitfalls, of course.

The Australian Norman O'Neill was the most

The great Don Bradman square cutting a ball from leg-spinner Roly Jenkins, playing against Worcestershire in 1948. From the position of wicket-keeper Hugo Yarnold, we can judge that the ball was about 18 inches outside the off stump and around waist-height. Ideal for the square cut.

powerful cutter I ever saw. He could cut the ball harder than any other stroke he played. I studied him on slow-motion film as he was particularly interesting to watch. With the ball a little wide of the stumps, he would initially move right across to the line and then in the last few feet would recoil, swaying away to make room for himself. His cut was a whipcrack of a shot with the ball rocketing away to the boundary.

The late Kenny Barrington was a very delicate and regular cutter. Good cutters tend to be back players and Kenny didn't too often move onto the front foot. He could play a neat, controlled little dab very well indeed.

Colin Milburn was another player I remember and admired for the way he rifled the ball square on the off side. It was in his case maybe half a cut and half a force off the back foot. Perhaps you should model yourself, less ambitiously, on slightly more orthodox players.

Gordon Greenidge is a marvellous player to watch. His square cut is quite superb. He has very, very good footwork – exemplary to my mind – and he's a sideways player. *Don't ignore this question of sideways play.* It's almost completely conditioned by the angle of the back foot. Keep it parallel with the crease, at right angles to the approach of the ball.

I used to be told to make absolutely sure of my sideways play by planting my back foot at 100–110 degrees from the line of the ball. And I must say it served me pretty well!

So many contributors in this book are rightly stressing the value of practice. Natural ability is a wonderful asset but refinement only comes from relentless practice.

I'm assuming you want to improve your cutting. So get into the net and ask someone to keep throwing the ball wide of your off stump, sufficiently short and with enough bounce for you to gain confidence in the use of the cut. Get used to bringing the bat up high and then coming down on the ball as it goes past you.

Bowling machines can also be invaluable, of course. Be on the look out for the ball rising at waist-height. If it's much higher than that, you are going to have difficulty controlling your cut. Always know when to leave well alone.

You must be wary of the ball swinging into you. As for the one going away, I argue that you can at least catch it up!

From the time the ball hits the pitch, you should be shaping for the cut. You'll be going up into the high sideways position I advocated. But the value is that you are still not committed – not until you have seen it coming off the ground. If it makes height dangerously, you should be able to leave it alone.

What about the line of fielders, maybe three slips and two gullys, waiting for you to cut? The cut is played downwards so there is no reason why the batsman need be inhibited. But at the same time, I always took the view that batting was at times a matter of pre-selection. Let me try to explain. If the fielding side has so many men in

England opener Tim Robinson plays a delicate late cut off a suitably short leg-break from Australian spinner Bob Holland. The shot, which is seldom played by most modern batsmen, appears to take wicket-keeper Wayne Phillips by surprise.

the slip area, clearly there are gaps elsewhere. It isn't a bad idea for the batsman to be thinking about driving rather more than cutting.

The good player notes how the field is set – and isn't going to fall for that. He isn't necessarily going to have anything to do with deliveries outside the off stump. He is prepared to wait for the bowler to make a mistake, so that the ball can then be on-driven or turned off the legs.

I'll end with a story rather against myself. It was that Old Trafford Test against the Australians in 1961 when we seemed to be perfectly positioned for a win. I was batting and their captain, Richie Benaud, switched to round the wicket with his leg-spinners. The intention was to slow England's scoring rate and I assumed he'd be bowling

Square Cut
Played to the ball pitching short, well outside the off stump.

1 The right foot goes back and across, pointing square to the off side. The left foot goes up on the toes, helping the body pivot; the left shoulder points up the wicket. The balance of the body is on the right leg. The bat is raised high, ready to swing down on the ball.

2 The hit is made, the right hand turning the face of the bat over to strike the ball down. Both arms have unhinged at the elbow. The weight of the body rocks back as the arms straighten and power is put into the shot.

3 The right wrist rolls over the left to complete the shot, keeping the ball down.

4 The right hand, having turned the bat blade over, continues in the follow-through over the left shoulder. The trunk turns with the swing.

outside leg stump, into the rough patches and the bowlers' foot marks.

It came as quite a surprise to me when Richie pitched one round about off stump and turning away. I tried to cut. But it was a little too close and it bounced. It got a faint nick and the great Wally Grout took the catch.

That was the end of the match for me. And that was the moment we lost the Test.

But cricket is a game of dangers and pitfalls. It is part of the appeal. What I have attempted to do is show you how to minimise the risks by wise technique – and to realise the added advantages of being a good back-foot player.

It isn't any accident, you know, that most efficient cutters are equally adept with the hook.

Late Cut

Played to the short-of-a-length ball when it is going past the batsman's right leg in the direction of third man. It should never be attempted against the inswinger or off-spinner.

1 The right foot moves back and outside the off stump; the left is up on its toes, giving a full pivot with the left shoulder pointing up the wicket. The balance of the body is on the right leg.

2 The hit is made, the right hand turning the face of the bat over in a whipping action, keeping the ball down. The eyes watch the ball on to the bat.

3 As the ball speeds away, the right hand continues to roll over the left until the face of the bat has turned completely over.

4 The right hand, still over the left, takes the bat on to complete the follow-through in a whipping movement across the body. The head remains steady throughout the shot.

DRIVING: PETER MAY

Peter May

Now we are talking of *style*. He had few peers in the post-war years. Whenever he picked up the bat, intent and schoolboy-high, it came down with purpose and elegance. If he was ever guilty of an untidy shot, few of us saw it. He scored 27,592 runs, at an average of 51, in a career that ended prematurely because of illness and business commitments. Most of those runs were beautifully fashioned.

Peter May first played for his country when he was twenty-one. It was a notable entry; he scored a hundred off a strong South African attack at Leeds in 1951. He went on to play sixty-six times for England – and he was captain in forty-one of those Tests. Often he dominated the England batting. His driving, especially through the on side, was a singular delight.

From Charterhouse days it was evident that he was going to be an exceptional cricketer. At Cambridge he was surrounded by batting talent: Sheppard, Dewes, Doggart. May made his debut for Surrey in 1950, and was captain of the county side from 1957–62. They were frequently heady days for Surrey – and for the tall, diffident man who led them.

That brings us to the paradox. He was fundamentally a shy, sensitive person. Yet as a captain, both of his county and his country, he could be surprisingly tough. He had a firm tactical sense and didn't believe in letting the opposition wriggle free. At all times he did it with a quiet, gracious charm. Those who didn't know him assumed he had many of the less personable qualities of some remote old-style amateurs. Nothing of the sort: he got on well with the pros, had a pleasant classless manner – there was no commission for him during his National Service – and, for his day, was modern in outlook.

There were eighty-five hundreds and five double centuries, the highest being an undefeated 285 against the West Indians at Edgbaston in 1957. Australians wryly claim that his finest batting was reserved for Sydney. May, modest and self-assured at the same time, wasn't lost to English cricket. His thoughtful, administrative skills have been valued and in 1982 he was appointed chairman of the Test selectors.

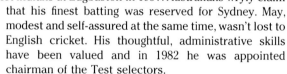

A lofted straight drive by Peter May, executed with perfect technique and timing. May was a superb driver of the ball anywhere in an arc between cover and mid-wicket, off either the front or back foot. The wicket-keeper is Roy Booth of Worcestershire.
(TPS/Central Press)

David Gower plays a flowing square drive to a ball from Geoff Lawson in the Lord's Test, 1985. This is not an easy shot to play against genuine pace, and no-one executes it better than Gower.

24

Driving

One of the things about driving is to know where you are going to hit the ball. It can be argued that it's only a good shot at cricket if it brings you runs.

So let's pause for a moment and analyse that. I think it makes a good deal of sense. However handsome your off-drive may be, it counts for nothing if it goes straight to a fielder. When I was batting I used to carry a picture in my mind of where the fielders were standing – and then I tried to avoid them!

I loved driving myself, and the off-drive is the most picturesque shot in cricket. Hundreds of coaches have told you how to pick the bat up to the top of the arc and then get your forward foot to the pitch of the ball with as full a stretch as possible. The bat follows through, the ball hits the middle of the bat and away it goes for a lovely boundary.

It all sounds fine, the perfect way to treat the nice half-volley. Many of you, I'm sure, do it with

South African opener Barry Richards stands up straight, weight solidly on the back foot, to drive a ball from fast bowler Bob Willis through the off-side field. In the slips are Alvin Kallicharran and Rohan Kanhai.

exquisite timing in the nets. Then you get out in the middle – and send one off-drive after another straight to the fielder. Nothing is more frustrating.

So one of your first basic priorities must be to miss the fielders, to find the gaps. The way to do this is let the ball come on a bit further. Don't hit it by the front foot but let it advance further, inside the front foot or the front heel. This lets you hit it squarer. Denis Compton was a master of that, of letting the ball come on to him. Len Hutton, too. They were two I tried to copy. Attempt to do what they did – let the bat come, as it were, from the inside. That way you are consciously trying to *place* the ball. You really have quite a wide arc, from mid-off to cover.

It's important knowing where the gaps are. The straight drive was a favourite of mine – and I knew that it offered me some kind of bonus. Once the bowler had released the ball and was running away, he had left a gap between himself and the stumps, and between the stumps and mid-on. And there was no fielder behind him.

Early in my career I worked out the value of scoring runs from the straight drive. The stumps, after all, weren't able to stretch out an arm to stop the ball once it had evaded the bowler as he followed through.

'When should I dare to loft my drives?' is a recurrent and fair question. It can be an exciting shot. But my guarded answer, usually said with a flicker of a smile, is: 'Probably not till you've made 100!' I was always reluctant myself to 'raise' my shots before I was very well set. Don Bradman hardly ever put the ball in the air.

The safest shot in cricket is the one that stays on the ground. The aim of every batsman must be to reduce the errors. So obviously it can be asking for trouble to hit the ball into the air. Whenever you lift that shot, you are taking something of a chance.

Having said that, it can be a very attractive drive, lofted over mid-off or extra cover. It still needs to be controlled. With added strength and confidence can come the sixes. Spectators love to see it.

Wally Hammond was one of the greatest off-drivers in the history of the game. He would play it both on the ground and in the air. But I advise the young player to use the lofted drive with caution. And make sure you know where the gaps are in the field.

We come now to the ON DRIVE. To my mind it's one of the hardest of all shots. You're actually having to hit a bit across the line.

From the way you are standing, facing the bowler with a sideways stance and front shoulder pointing towards him, you are theoretically avoiding any temptation to hit across the line. Now, for the on-drive, you are having rather to depart from this.

You'll need to 'open yourself out' – to open the front foot and point the toe towards mid-on. But this is the secret. As long as you keep your head absolutely still and right in line, you will be all right. You can then let the bat come through in that line and you won't be vulnerable.

It's a good time to emphasise the value of keeping the head still. Take a look at many of the truly great players. Notice how long they remain

With masterly technique, Geoff Boycott on-drives a half-volley from Greg Chappell in the Headingley Test of 1977 to reach his 100th hundred in first-class cricket. David Hookes and Rick McCosker look on.

motionless before making their stroke. It's often said that the greater the player, the later he will play his stroke – and it will still seem as if he has all the time in the world.

The on-drive is a very productive shot and I was lucky enough to play it pretty well. The West Indians are powerful leg-side players and it is always unwise bowling on leg stump or even middle stump to someone like Viv Richards, for instance. As a general rule, the place to bowl is off stump and outside. Things haven't really changed over the years.

So far I've been talking about driving off the front foot. But it can be just as exhilarating off the back. Clyde Walcott used to drive off the back foot as powerfully as anyone off the front. I agree with others in this book that the best batsmen in the history of cricket have been outstanding backfoot players.

One of the problems I notice among some present-day batsmen is that they half commit themselves to the forward shot – even before the ball has actually arrived.

It has always struck me that if a batsman plays back, he still leaves himself with time and the option of going forward. *If you go forward, you can't change your mind and come back.* So it means that by playing back, in effect you give yourself two chances.

Frankly I loved going up onto my toes to drive off the back foot. I didn't hook myself and the drive was my main source of runs when I went back.

The potential driver of the ball needs to make up his mind fairly early about length. If the ball comes up above waist-height, it will be more difficult to control. Nor will you be able to hit the ball with the middle of the bat. You will take the ball up on the splice instead and the shot will lack power.

Whereas the hook and the pull are played in the air and arguably dangerous for the batsman, the drives should ideally be played along the ground. Look for the gaps . . . and wait for the umpire to signal four!

Of the modern English players, David Gower was particularly impressive with his driving in 1985. Tim Robinson produced some fine drives off his legs. Graham Gooch can drive on both sides of the wicket. Mike Gatting and Ian Botham drive well. Earlier, Colin Cowdrey was a magnificent driver – he always appeared to have so much time to play the ball. His timing was impeccable and because of that, he just seemed to stroke the ball to the boundary.

Get out in the nets, even if you know you'll never quite emulate the top players . . . Have someone throw half-volleys to you. Left leg forward, swing the bat through, and keep the ball on the ground. As your drive improves along with your confidence, move your colleague farther and farther back until he can actually bowl at you from 22 yards.

As a driver, you are hunting for runs. But never let your concentration lapse. Watch the ball intently – on a sunny day, you may even see it spinning in the air. Don't be frightened to take a couple of paces down the wicket to the slow bowler. Remember the basic rules at the same time.

Have confidence to go through with the stroke and not stop on it. Follow through just like a golfer does. He doesn't stop halfway through. And nor does a golfer start with his club in the air. I was always taught to pick the bat up from the crease – it just doesn't seem quite right to me for a batsman to start with his bat in the air. But then, that's a bit of a hobby horse of mine!

I mentioned just now the need to have the confidence of going through with the shot. It reminds me of the Birmingham Test in 1957, where I was in a big partnership with Colin Cowdrey. When I went in second time, we needed 260 to save an innings defeat. It looked impossible. Sonny Ramadhin had been in fine form in the first innings and I hadn't been in long before he pitched one on off stump. I wasn't sure which way it was going – you could never be absolutely sure with Sonny. But I middled it perfectly and it scorched through extra cover for four. There had been a fleeting moment when I wondered whether I should go through with the drive. The result was a psychological triumph for me. I went on to make 285 and Colin 150.

If you're having sudden problems with your driving, never be afraid to ask for advice. Even a great golfer like Jack Nicklaus would go to his coach if he felt there was something wrong with his swing. There were times when I used to ask our coach at Surrey, Andrew Sandham, to stand behind the net and tell me what I was doing wrong. At different times I was moving before the ball was bowled, and then I had a tendency to open my stance.

You'll be given all sorts of advice, of course, most of it well-meaning. Always listen. But remember, there is only one person who can put a technical problem right – *yourself.*

A classic cover-drive by Tom Graveney, one of the most elegant strokemakers to have graced the game. Particularly strong off the front foot, Graveney used his long reach to turn many a good length ball into a driveable half-volley.

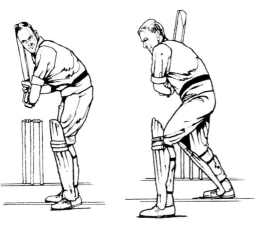

Cover Drive

Played to the overpitched ball outside the off stump. The shot can be risky since it is played across the line of the ball in the direction of cover point.

1 The left foot goes forward and alongside the line of the ball, the toes pointing towards cover. The weight goes over the left leg. The bat is raised high with the left shoulder towards the line of the oncoming ball. The head is steady, the eyes watching the ball in its flight down the wicket.

2 As the leg goes forward the bat commences its downward swing, coming from the line of the leg stump towards the ball wide of the off stump. At this stage, the left hand has the major part in directing the swing of the bat. The left shoulder is still pointed towards the line of the ball.

3 The face of the bat is square on, aiming towards cover point. Both hands are working together. The swing of the bat has been accelerated with the uncocking of the left wrist. The left arm is almost fully unhinged. The right hand is behind the handle and still slightly cocked, putting the power into the shot.

4 Up on the toes of the right foot. The bat has swung out and away, following through in the direction of the shot, and the wrists have turned over in a natural movement, following the punch through with the right hand in making the hit. The shoulders and hips open up as the right hand comes through.

On Drive

Played to the ball pitching on the half-volley length, on or just outside the leg stump.

1 The bat is raised as the left leg prepares to go out alongside the line of the ball, and up to the half-volley.

2 The weight moves over the left leg. Both wrists are cocked and both elbows bent, with the left hand leading the down swing of the bat in a line from outside the off stump towards the on-side ball. The right knee is bent inwards, turning the right hip round.

3 The bat face comes square on to the ball. The left arm unhinges, and the right arm straightens as the right hand uncocks to put the power into the shot. The right heel comes off the ground, helping the body balance to go forward over the front leg. The trunk is almost square on towards the ball.

4 The shoulders turn with the follow-through of the right hand. The head stays steady, the eyes watching the ball on its way.

Straight Drive (off the back foot)

Played to a short (but not too short) straight delivery, aiming to hit the ball past the bowler to either side of the stumps.

1 Take the bat up high with a full cocking of the wrists, the right foot going back as far as possible towards the middle stump and pointing to the off side. Go up on the toes of the left foot, helping to lift the left shoulder and to shift the body balance on to the back foot.

2 The weight remains on the back foot. Coming up on the toes of the front foot assists the hands to punch the ball away. The left hand is firm, controlling the swing in the direction of the shot. The right hand administers the hit. The eyes watch the ball over the left hand.

3 Completion of the shot. The trunk opens up as the right hand follows through in a full swing.

OPENING THE INNINGS:
BOBBY SIMPSON

Bobby Simpson

Bobby Simpson was the Aussie who played fifty-two times for his country, retired to get on with a business career and then ten years later when into his forties came back as captain in another ten Tests. It was seen as a rescue act. Establishment cricket in Australia had been denuded by WSC.

He was quite an individualist. It was evident in his approach to captaincy. He knew how to get the best out of his players; he nursed and coaxed the rawer recruits with genuine skill. There was the familiar, distinctive sight of him, too: waiting, hands on knees, in the slips. Those strong fingers spilled very little. But in his individualistic fashion, he worked out ways to ease his intense concentration and was able to relax until the ball was actually on its way.

Few would have called him charismatic – or even a particularly imaginative player. But he had gritty durability and great application. His fitness was legendary. He could sweat all day and never wilt. He had the muscles of a lumberjack and the other players envied his remarkable stamina.

Bobby Simpson wasn't the most handsome batsman who ever opened the innings for his country. He had a fine square cut, however, his straight drive could be a cracker and his on-drive was in the Australian tradition. He was also a stayer. Playing for New South Wales in 1963–4 he scored 800 runs in four innings and no-one was going to get him away from the crease. At Old Trafford, he stayed 12 hours 42 minutes, more than two days, in scoring 311 and making the Ashes safe.

He made his Test debut, against the South Africans, over Christmas in 1957 as a middle-order batsman. It was Neil Harvey who told him he should be opening the innings. His dogged character brought him sixty centuries. He captained Australia in thirty-nine of his sixty-two Tests. And he did it by example.

Bobby Simpson had all the attributes of a good Test opener: a sound technique against fast bowling, model patience and concentration, and the determination to play a long innings. He was also one of the best takers of a quick single in the game. Recalled out of retirement at the age of forty-one to captain Australia against India, he scored over 500 runs in the series – including this classic off-drive for four.
(TPS/Central Press)

Opening the Innings

Opening batsmen are the explorers of cricket. Virtually every time that they go out to bat, they are entering unknown and often unfriendly territory.

While the unknown for them is only 22 yards, this terrain has proved on occasions to be almost as unpredictable as some of the unexplored areas confronted by our great adventurers of the past; and while there may not be hostile natives with various weapons to face, a 5½ ounce red missile can inflict almost as much damage. But like the adventurers of the past, good openers know that successful forages into the unknown can bring great personal rewards and success for their team – and, at Test level, for their country. Failure, on the other hand, carries with it personal disappointment and hardship for the side.

Australian cricket for some years has suffered through a lack of successful openers, and it is no coincidence that this period has proved to be one of Australia's worst eras in the game. Although I may be biased, I feel the opening positions are the most important spots in cricket; and while facing high-speed bowling or cunning operators of the new ball may not be everyone's cup of tea, it can be immensely rewarding and not nearly as difficult as many would have us believe.

It also probably carries more satisfaction, though not perhaps enjoyment, for a job well done than any other position in cricket. After all, it would take a masochist to find pleasure in facing a tear-away bowler operating at around 90mph with a drawn cricket ball at twenty-two paces. But it is a job that can be carried out successfully, providing the person who fills that position desperately wants the job and has done his homework.

Of all positions in the batting line-up, the opening berth requires that the batsman knows his own strengths and limitations and has a clear and concise view on how to play within both. It also requires that he understands the strengths and weaknesses of the opening bowlers, and that he is prepared to be adaptable to counter or control them.

But the major requirement to be a successful opener is to have a total understanding with, and commitment to, your partner.

Obviously it is vital for all budding openers to have a sound basic technique which can withstand the mental pressure exerted by a fast bowler, who seems hell bent on knocking your head off or wicket down. The more correct the technique is, and the greater the understanding the opener has of his own game, the more likely will be his success.

All batsmen, and openers in particular, must assess before each match the opposition bowlers and the most likely way they can get you out. For instance, a left-hand swing bowler normally tries to get a right-hand batsman lbw playing back to an inswinger, or caught behind with one that leaves him. Armed with this information, a right-hand batsman should be trying to push forward whenever possible to nullify these tactics. Obviously he wouldn't push forward to everything, but if the 'computer' between the ears is alerted it will react quicker when called upon. All bowlers have a most likely way to get a batsman out and this knowledge must be fed into the computer, along with the best way to combat their tactics, before each match so that batting instincts are pre-fired.

But while technique and skills and courage are all necessary requirements of an opening batsman, it is almost impossible to succeed without a compatible partner.

If I had to pass on just one tip about how to be a successful opener, it would be: *Get to the bowler's end as much as possible.* If you are at the bowler's end you can't get out! If both batsmen are working on the same principle and rotating the strike, the bowlers have less chance of exerting pressure or operating to their game plan.

That is what a partnership is all about and why it is so important to have a compatible mate. Opening bowlers are more often seen off through strike rotation, which puts *them* under pressure and produces loose deliveries, than any other form of attack.

While opening the batting may not be fun, it is seldom dull. Those 22 yards of unexplored territory, and the new ball, see to that.

Undoubtedly, a cricket pitch is the most discussed area in the world. At almost every game it is scrutinized, debated and assessed, generally without much success, and even today after thirty-odd years of looking down on such territory, I still can't tell precisely how a pitch will play – and I

Indian opening batsman Sunil Gavaskar attempts to score from a defensive stroke by angling the bat and steering the ball wide of the field.

The pressure is on Geoff Boycott as he resolutely defends against the pace of Dennis Lillee and his threatening cordon of close fielders.

doubt whether anyone else can either. What I do know however is that runs can be scored on almost any pitch, providing the batsman treats every ball on merit and doesn't go looking for a minefield.

New balls are also always a challenge – no two play the same, not even from the same box. They can be affected by manufacturing, atmospheric conditions or the pitch itself. And like the pitch, they are impossible to pick. So openers may as well forget about it and get on with the job of playing every ball on merit.

To sum up:

To be a successful opening batsman you must, first of all, have an appetite for the job. It is no good going in first if you would really rather be batting lower down the order.

You must not be afraid of fast bowling. And you must possess quick reflexes, a good eye and the batting techniques not only to defend against pace but to attack it as well when the opportunity arises.

You must have the right temperament for an opener and not be overawed by the occasion, or unnerved by the heightened tension that normally accompanies the start of a match or a new innings.

You must have a sense of responsibility. This of course can be said of any batsman, but the opening pair have the particular responsibility of trying to get the innings established by seeing off the new ball and giving their fellow batsmen something substantial to build on. An opening batsman isn't there to throw his wicket away by playing irresponsible shots.

You must have patience, determination and the ability to concentrate, all in good measure. These, along with the correct batting skills, and your share of good luck, should get you off to a good start.

The basis of Barry Richards' superb technique was a straight bat. Here he gets right behind the ball to play an immaculate defensive stroke off the back foot.

Playing the Inswinger off the Front Foot

1 Go up on the toes of the right foot, the sole pivoting to turn the body. The left foot goes out towards the line of the ball. The right wrist is fully cocked. The eyes watch the ball about to pitch. The weight is well over the left leg. The left arm is bent, the left hand leading the swing of the bat. To get the face of the bat to the ball, the batsman must turn the shoulders with the forehead towards the line of the ball.

2 The ball is played away. The eyes watch it over the left hand, which still leads the bat. The right hand is behind the handle. The weight remains over the left leg.

Playing the Inswinger off the Back Foot

1 Adopt the open stance when facing the inswinger, the left foot pointing in the direction of extra cover, the hips and shoulders slightly opened up. The right foot goes back towards the middle-and-off, and the left moves back to join it as the bat swings down from outside the off stump. The trunk begins to turn with the movement of the bat.

2 The ball pitches, the eyes watching it over the left arm. The weight is well over the braced right leg. The hands bring the bat down, the left hand leading; the face of the bat about to come square on to the ball. The bat is held high with arms bent, in readiness to play the ball bouncing up off the pitch.

3 The left hand, in front of the right, angles the bat to keep the ball down. The face of the bat has turned towards the on side to meet the ball just in front of the right leg. The right hand is relaxed. The trunk and shoulders turn with the stroke.

Playing the Outswinger off the Front Foot

1 The left foot goes out towards the line of the oncoming ball, the bat having started the down swing simultaneously. The left knee bends, taking the weight of the body. Both arms are bent; the right wrist is fully cocked. The left hand leads the bat, angling it backwards.

2 The face of the bat goes through towards the off side in the upright position. The left hand is in front of the bat, keeping it upright, as the right hand behind the handle pushes the ball away. The eyes watch the ball go off the bat. The trunk opens up. The right elbow stays close to the side.

Playing the Outswinger off the Back Foot

1 The first move must be made with the object of getting the face of the bat behind the line of the stumps. The right foot goes back towards the off stump; the shoulder sideways on. The weight is on the back leg. The bat goes up to the higher pick-up position, travelling up to a line over middle and leg stumps. The eye-line goes past the left shoulder, following the oncoming ball.

2 The ball is about to be played. The left foot has moved back to join the right foot simultaneously with the commencement of the down swing of the bat. The hips open slightly, but the shoulder stays sideways on. The right arm is well into the right side, both wrists uncocking. The left hand controls the swing of the bat which remains angled backwards – the face square on to the approaching ball.

3 Hips and shoulders open as the hands take the bat out to meet the ball, the face square on to the outswing line of the ball. The right arm hugs the right side. The forward thrust of the right arm close to the body opens the shoulders, but the left hand leading the bat to keep it angled down stops the shoulders from opening as much as the hips. The balance of the body is retained on the braced right leg.

BUILDING AN INNINGS:
COLIN COWDREY

Colin Cowdrey

It seems outrageous, certainly impertinent, to suggest that he might have done better. Why, he played 114 times for England and scored 107 hundreds. Why, he compiled more than 42,000 runs and once hit 307 against South Australia at Adelaide. Why, his timing was the nearest thing to perfection in the first-class game. So why? Why did his admirers presume to criticise?

Colin Cowdrey was the definitive nice guy. He lacked that touch of malevolent granite that at times would have kept him even longer at the wicket. There were the occasions when he became introspective at the crease, failing to take the game to the bowler. He should have been more dominant, more defiant – but that wasn't his nature. He was a courteous and charming chap who found it difficult to unfurl his colours and ride out with a flourish to meet his enemy.

He was brilliant enough to crack records. Yet there could so easily have been more of them. At the age of thirteen he was playing for Tonbridge at Lord's. By 1950, still only seventeen, he was playing for Kent, and people were asking excitedly where it would end. In all, until his retirement in 1976, he played 402 times for his county. That represented many great innings – and always a superb and envied technique.

He captained Kent from 1957–71 and led England in twenty-seven Tests. Significantly he was never appointed higher than vice-captain for the tours of Australia. If the selectors suspected his fibre, in the mental sense, they had no doubts about his courage and commitment. That was why they summoned him, at very short notice, to face up to Lillee and Thomson when he was forty-two and out of practice.

His idol was Hutton, upon whom he based his approach. Colin Cowdrey didn't go in for ostentatious attacking shots. He simply didn't need them in his extensive and polished repertoire. The statistics are impressive as they stand; so are the memories, of what he did on the West Indies tour of 1959–60, or at Melbourne. Perhaps some of us will never be satisfied.

Colin Cowdrey on the attack during his innings of 71 for England against the Rest of the World at Edgbaston in 1970. (Left) The spinners are on and Cowdrey goes on to the front foot to a ball wide of the off stump and strokes it handsomely to the boundary.

(Right) His half-century behind him, Cowdrey picks up a delivery from Intikhab Alam and hoists it over the ropes for six. Deryck Murray of West Indies is behind the stumps, with South Africa's Peter Pollock taking evasive action at silly mid-on.

Building an Innings

It may seem odd – but I can't help making a comparison with snooker. The similarities of building an innings and a snooker break occur to me every time I see Steve Davis or one of his brilliant rivals on the television.

Just think about it for a moment. A snooker break is painstakingly constructed. Thought is given to the shots ahead as well as the one being currently played. The top players don't recklessly go for everything. There are occasions when they opt for a defensive shot, so making things harder and increasing the frustration for the opposition.

What is the first thing I think about in my resolve to build an innings? It may appear rather too obvious. The fact is that my primary job is to *survive the first ball*.

Don't reject my advice as being too basic. I can't over-stress how important it is. There are so many aspects. You are probably going to be nervous – and *it does take time for the eye to adjust*.

People used to comment on how slowly the great Don Bradman took to walk to the wicket. He would look up at the sun a couple of times and then stroll out. He was a highly intelligent man and his slow walk, as he conditioned himself to the light, was quite deliberate.

Ideally a batsman should get out in the open air before his innings but, certainly in the county game, that isn't often practicable. Going back to Bradman, he used to say that the relatively soft light of England was easier than Australia for the new batsman.

The first ball is fraught with dangers for the unwary. So the batsman must be very much in control. His preparation for it is both mental and physical.

Wally Hammond told me that one way to offset any nervousness was to put the bottom batting hand on the top of the woodwork. That would prove a steadying influence. I could see that if my hands were wandering around at the top of the handle, the bat would be floating around like a feather. It also helped to control the backlift.

I've often watched nervous youngsters facing the first two or three balls. Their feet are all over the place and their bat is up around their ears. They are out of control and don't really know what they are doing.

A few more words about the first ball. It takes a lot of analysing. So take your time over guard. I'm not encouraging you to show-off, sticking your chest out and irking the bowler to the extent that he'll let one fly 8mph faster than usual!

But don't be afraid to take a calculated look back beyond the bowler, to get a 'feel' of the background. By now you know where the fielders are and are willing yourself to survive the opening delivery. Now I come to the final rule for this early stage of the innings – *you must switch on and focus totally on the ball itself*.

It must be admitted that many batsmen, often nervous, fail to watch it very closely. They vaguely see a chap coming up to bowl and the arm go over. And they go through the motions of playing something red. I know – I've done it myself!

I wouldn't dissuade any batsman from taking early advantage of bad deliveries. Jack Hobbs was always on the look-out for a loosener and relished hitting the first ball for four. On the other hand, I must sound a few words of common-sense caution. The batsman does need to be conscious of playing the line of the stumps.

Unfortunately, there's this sad tendency because of nervousness of playing a ridiculous shot to something very wide. That means you are out of control. A disciplined shot off a full toss back past the bowler, wide of mid-on or through extra cover, for instance, shows no loss of concentration and control.

Avoid that awful slash off the back foot when you are not quite in. I can remember being out several times trying to hook and getting a glove to it. That's maddening – what a waste! You want to be in for three hours and are needlessly out in the first minute . . .

I make no excuse for devoting so much of my advice to the opening balls you receive. Get that hand down firmly on the top of the bat – and make the bat go down the line of the middle stump. These extra little disciplines give you added confidence and more time.

It becomes almost an obsession for some players to get off the mark. It never really bothered me – perhaps it should have more. Once in a University match against MCC at Lord's I got a pair on a beautiful wicket. In the first innings I was out to a blinder in the gully third ball. Then I spent twenty minutes, in the second innings, whacking balls to mid-off and extra cover. With the confidence of youth I turned down singles – and then I was out. Maybe my patience was counter-productive.

Targets are quite important in building an innings. They should never be too ambitious. One run should be the first target, then five and ten. Certainly I was a target man in the early part of the innings. It probably isn't quite so important for an attacking genius like Viv Richards.

I have always argued that it's vital *to bat in pairs*. This is part of the fun of the game and is also a necessary part of teamwork. It's terribly important to chat together, between overs. Talk about the bowler and the state of the match. Talk about your immediate aims. Your partner, from his particular vantage point, will see things you utterly missed. It happens that batsmen are concentrating to such an extent that they overlook the obvious.

You should help each other all the time. It may be that one of you is bogged down and the opposing captain is putting added pressure on you because of it. That again is when your partner can sometimes help. You must be prepared to take your time and yet make a positive effort to keep the score ticking over.

For all sorts of reasons there are days when we are happier playing the slow rather than the quick bowlers – or the other way round. Maybe we have run into a few problems using our feet to the slow bowlers and have lost some confidence. That is when the partner can once more come to the rescue.

When I was flown out to join the England side against Australia in 1974 I lacked match practice. I was at No 3 and was soon in, facing Thomson and Lillee who were very fast and downwind! I soon realised that David Lloyd was taking more than his share of the pace men. I apologised to him and said we must break it up.

David said he wasn't in too much trouble and was happy to keep playing the fearsome pair for the time being. He felt it was reasonable as I had only just flown out from England. That, to my mind, was a very generous piece of cricket from David Lloyd.

It is a team game and the batsman must always be aware of the needs of his team. There are occasions when Geoff Boycott has made enormous scores and has yet left his captain little room to manoeuvre. Geoff would no doubt point to his marvellous statistics and defend his action.

Calmness is a valuable quality in building the innings. It's useful to be able to stand back and assess what is happening. There is a fascination about compiling an innings. It calls for intelligence, discrimination, awareness of what is needed by your team . . . and a determination not to allow the bowler to dominate you.

The one-day match (and the same often applies in local competitive cricket) is apt to place different demands on you. Your technique has at times to be revised and there has to be a measure of improvisation. Yet the best players still have scope to build an innings. I can think of one classic example by Derek Randall at Lord's – and I have no doubt that you'll see many more in the course of a season.

Let me finally reiterate a couple of points. The building of an innings is not as personal as it sounds – it relies on two players rather than one.

Tom Graveney was a tremendous operator and somewhat underrated. I loved being in with him. He had a good thinking head. He was so talented at placing the ball and keeping the score going. The two of us were able to run effortlessly together. That's another consideration – the easy ability to run between the wickets. It doesn't always happen, my goodness, no!

The record books will also show how often I found myself batting with Peter May for England. Again it was a perfect partnership. It was always a matter of enjoyment. And, of course, it was without rivalry. There are times when rivalry among the two batsmen at the wicket becomes evident. The result is that it is inclined to work against them. It turns into a bonus for the fielding side.

And just a last word about those nerves. I see nothing wrong in making a complete break, mentally, between overs – even, on occasions, between deliveries. Godfrey Evans used to be marvellous at that. Have a quick natter at the wicket. 'Where shall we go for a meal after the match?' . . . 'Feel like a film? . . .'

That gives you the opportunity to switch right back, in an intense and positive way, for the next ball you have to receive.

FAST BOWLING: FRED TRUEMAN

Fred Trueman

Fiery Fred, that's what they called him. He rather basked in that kind of description. He remained strong on expletives and bouncers. He occasionally told the authorities where they got off. He drove one or two captains close to distraction. And he steadfastly believed there was only one place for the batsman: back in the pavilion.

He was gruff, granity, warm-hearted and funny. The Yorkshire crowds loved to see him steaming in, nostrils aflame. His hostility was short-lived. At the end of play he was gregarious, dispensing earthy epigrams, wisecracking with fellow cricketers and supporters. He was the No 1 character of his day and there were the matches when he felt duty-bound to reveal that flailing bat. But remember he hit three hundreds.

Fred Trueman was, of course, a fine bowler. There was the genuine pace which could be a quite fearsome sight to a naturally timorous batsman. The ball would bite and gather speed off the ground, it would swing away. His yorker became a dastardly addition to his range.

He bowled his heart out sixty-seven times for England and ended with 307 wickets, having been the first to pass 300. In his first series, against India, he frightened the life out of a few of their batsmen and took 29 wickets. Many others quaked after that: mostly batsmen. In truth, the Trueman temperament softened and matured.

His career ended in the late sixties and in that time he captured 2,304 wickets at an average of 18.29. Twelve times he took 100 in a season. He was proud of his four hat-tricks, a sentiment hardly shared by Nottinghamshire who were on the receiving end all but once. He had the speech, the gait and the resilient spirit of a Yorkshire miner. But he loved the fresh air, particularly the bracing breezes of Dover where once, above the cliffs, he took 8–28 against Kent before lunch. He looked on it as a good way to work up a thirst.

Fred Trueman: the action of a great fast bowler. The left arm is straight, with the head still and the eyes looking over the left shoulder. The weight is being transferred from the right foot to the left leg, with the right arm poised for the final arc of the delivery.

Fast Bowling

I get pretty annoyed when I hear how someone or other is supposedly going to be turned into a fast bowler. Believe me, it just doesn't happen. Fast bowlers are born and not made. Some people can bowl fast, some can't. If you haven't got the natural gifts, you'll never be coached, talked and persuaded into it.

That brings me to my second point. If you can bowl fast, you must also WANT to bowl fast. That means making use of all your aggression. There has never been a successful fast bowler who

Dennis Lillee on his last tour of England in 1981. Some of the pace has gone, but the aggressive instinct and magnificent bowling action are still very much in evidence.

didn't have fire in his belly. In other words, you must have a natural hate of batsmen.

Perhaps I should quickly explain. I'm not suggesting that you should hate the batsman as a person. You must hate him in the sense of wanting to get him out – to dominate him, to be the top dog. So, remember, *you must be a fast bowler in heart, mind and body.*

You might as well pack up if you're not dedicated to hard work. Fast bowling can be very hard work. You must be prepared to try to bowl the opposition out on all sorts of wickets, even the very slow ones. It's great when you find yourself with a nice, bouncy wicket – but it doesn't happen very often. Groundsmen are apt to slow the wicket down if the visiting team have a useful quickie!

There's a misplaced glamour about fast bowlers. They tend to win the big matches for you, it's true. There is something about the strike bowler in full flight. But don't forget all the sweat and hard toil that goes into it.

Let us get on to basics. The pace man needs a good, rhythmic action. And no-one will ever alter my view that it should be *sideways on.* In that way, you get the whole power of the body from the hips into the delivery. You get the long arc, the swing of the arm, which releases the ball. You acquire the natural pivot and body action that helps you to obtain movement through the air.

Maurice Leyland, the great Yorkshire batsman, always used to tell me that the ball leaving the bat and swinging away was the most difficult to play. I'll go along with that. Just take a look in the record books. The great wicket-takers were all bowlers who could make the ball leave the bat – the leg-spinners and outswingers like Dennis Lillee, Ray Lindwall and . . . well, yes, myself.

As a fast bowler, you must learn to use the crease. Be able to bowl by the side of the stumps, wicket-to-wicket, in the middle of the crease and wide of the crease. *Bowling is all about angles.* If you can 'angle' your batsman, you've got a good chance of getting him out.

Many times, for example, I've delivered from close to the stumps and pitched on off and middle. The ball has gone straight on, the batsman has played and missed and I've knocked over the off stump. Back in the pavilion, the batsman says in despair: 'However do you play one like that?' All I've done is 'angled' him. In effect, I've got him on the wrong foot.

Another way of obtaining this necessary angle is to bowl the away-swinger from wide of the crease or the inswinger from close to the stumps. The result is that the batsman defends his wicket against the ball that looks as though it's coming into him and then suddenly leaves him – or against the one that appears to be going outside his off stump, then swings in late to trap him lbw.

There's plenty of advice to be offered about how to grip the ball for swing bowling. Frankly, I didn't get my movement from my grip. I did it in a completely different way. *I achieved away-swing naturally* by making sure my left shoulder was pointing down the wicket and my left arm pointed towards where fine leg should be.

I knew when I was bowling well. It felt easy, and I could see the top of my shoulder out of the corner of my left eye. When I delivered the ball, my arm came up and over and across my body – with my head perfectly still, which is so important – and finished on the outside of my left leg.

Here's another strong argument for bowling sideways on. *That way you hide the ball.* The

Michael Holding, at his peak one of the fastest bowlers ever, combines grace, hostility and power as he smoothly accelerates to the wicket and leaps into the delivery stride.

batsman doesn't pick it up until the arm is practically into the delivery position. And remember that the batsman often doesn't like to play forward. He prefers sitting on the back foot, lengthening the delivery and letting the ball come to him. *As a bowler, it's up to you to work all these things out.*

Get to know a batsman's strengths and weaknesses, and put them firmly in the memory bank. We'll assume you've acquired a nice economical and rhythmic run-up and that the rhythm and balance come together at the moment of actual delivery. Now is the time to use your head.

Maybe the batsman is a naturally front-foot player. If that's the case, you can bowl a little bit shorter. Perhaps he's a back-foot man – if so, pitch the ball up. If he's a strong on-side batsman, aim at his off stump. If he's best through the off side,

Richard Hadlee generates hostile lift and pace off a relatively short run. His principal weapon is a devastating outswinger, fast and late.

go for his leg stump or middle and leg. Always attempt to play on his weaknesses. That is why it's important to be aware of his natural first movement, backwards or forwards. Watch the batsman intently as you deliver.

Let me come on to variation. Your job is to outthink the batsman. Keep him guessing. It's pointless to bowl as fast as you possibly can every time you run up to the wicket. You wouldn't last long that way, I'm telling you! Disguise that quicker one. Ray Lindwall and Dennis Lillee did it so well – and I like to think I did, too. I'm talking of the ball that is half a yard faster. It's the one to let go now and again.

In the same way, be selective with bouncers. They are a legitimate weapon and use them by all means. I certainly did! *But know when . . .*

To me there is far too much short-pitched bowling in the modern game. The artistry of fast bowling is disappearing. In its place is the surfeit of balls banged in short, to come up around the batsman's ribs and shoulders. That to me is wrong.

Psychology comes into it. Some advantage can often be gained by showing the batsman that you can bowl a bouncer. The batsman at the bowler's end is also watching, of course – and it's no bad thing to get him a bit wary, as well. But it seems to me often pointless to bowl short indiscriminately.

Think about it for a moment. If the batsman can't hook and just keeps ducking, you are wasting your time and your energy. Nothing is being achieved. The batsmen who can't hook OR duck, and the batsmen who CAN hook are the ones who should be tested with the occasional bouncer.

Try to be on the look-out all the time. Check the batsman's initial movement and where he's gripping the bat. If the batsman has a top hand a little bit round, you can draw the conclusion that he can't hit through the off side. His strength is probably through mid-on and mid-wicket. So bowl at off and middle and concentrate on away-swing. He may hit across the line and make it easier for you.

The yorker, as Joel Garner discovered long ago, can be a valuable wicket-taker. My own rule used to be to aim at the base of the stumps, leg and middle. The idea is to pitch right into the batsman's feet, tucking him up. Maybe the batsman has been hitting you – so why not pitch that ball so close to him that he hasn't room to swing the bat.

A fast bowler needs wise captaincy. He should never be over-bowled. Say five or six overs, then a rest, and back again later for another spell. But, of course, it all depends on the circumstances of the match, and the conditions.

Because of the tremendous physical stress put on fast bowling, there is always a risk of injury. I must say that I sent down so many overs myself

Controlled aggression from Craig McDermott. The young Australian has three of the essential requirements for a successful fast bowler: a strong physique, a willingness to work hard, and an insatiable appetite for wickets.

that I reckon I 'bowled myself fit'. I never once pulled a muscle. I'm convinced that many of the injuries can be attributed to awkward actions.

One of the obstacles, I used to think, was pain. You had to grit your teeth and go through the pain barrier. Until you did, you were not a complete fast bowler. That still holds true. *Bowling fast is hard work – and painful.* And very, very rewarding.

It can also be pretty frustrating, I must admit, if someone like Viv Richards is really going. But again, observation is important. His first movement is when his front foot goes across the stumps. He has in effect to bring the bat round the front pad. So I'd always be attempting to swing the ball away from him.

I'm not suggesting potential young fast bowlers around the country are going to have to face one of the great batsmen of the modern era! But I'm making the point that there is always something to learn and act upon.

What do I think of the present-day pace bowlers? Overlooking the West Indies battery and that fine New Zealand new ball man Richard Hadlee, I see Stephen Andrew, of Hampshire, as one of the best prospects. I'll be interested to see if he gets more scope with the county and lives up to his promise. And Down Under, of course, there's Craig McDermott, who bowled very well in England in 1985 and showed that he's not afraid of hard work.

Fast Bowling

To bowl fast the bowling arm must swing over as quickly as possible. To achieve this, the trunk must do a rapid twist and turn. The run-up should be accelerating so that the quickest point will be at the take-off jump towards the bowling crease.

1 The final stride to the crease: the mid-air position just before landing. The right leg is going past the left and is about to land with the foot pointing square to the off side. The trunk is turning towards the sideways-on position. The left arm is reaching as high as possible. The eyes look over the left shoulder. The head is steady.

2 The right leg is braced. The right arm has gone forward and down and is about to commence the upward swing. The left leg is high and bent, ready to go forward with the forward swing of the left arm.

3 The rapid turn of the trunk and hips means a more complete follow-through over the left leg. The right arm follows the left arm round the body. The hips do a complete turn, the trunk dips low. The forehead is towards the batsman.

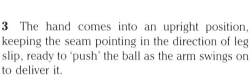

Right Arm Inswinger

1 The first two fingers are angled across the seam. The thumb grips the ball underneath, pressing against the seam, with the third and fourth fingers in support.

2 Just before release. The wrist is cocked backwards, the chest is well open.

3 The hand comes into an upright position, keeping the seam pointing in the direction of leg slip, ready to 'push' the ball as the arm swings on to deliver it.

4 The right hand stays in the 'release' position, the right arm swings past the right side. Head steady, the eyes follow the ball down the wicket.

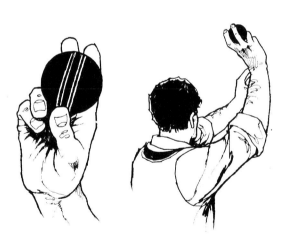

Right Arm Outswinger

1 Hold the ball with the first two fingers angled across the seam. The thumb is underneath on the seam, the third and fourth fingers support.

2 The position of the hands and arms on arriving at the crease. The right wrist is cocked backwards.

3 Just before releasing the ball. The hand is now upright. The movement of the trunk turning towards the batsman brings the ball round so that the seam is pointing in the direction of first slip.

4 The right side has come through, with the right leg about to step over the left. The hand keeps the 'release' position. The bowling arm swings forward and down and across the body to chase the left arm around the left side.

LEFT-ARM PACE: JOHN LEVER

John Lever

Many county cricketers would nominate John Lever as our most consistently penetrative and successful native pace bowler of recent years. The Essex captain Keith Fletcher would find no fault with that statement. After all, the considerable influence of this left-arm bowler can be detected very clearly in the county's collection of trophies.

In 1983 he took 106 wickets; in 1984 he took 116. Such form by a bowler in his mid-thirties inevitably prompted the question as to whether he might still have been of value to England. The speculation was pointless, of course; he was then banned for playing in South Africa. The talented Lever had made a calculated decision. He had been chosen for only one Test during the 1981–2 tour of India and he suspected that his appearances for England were virtually at an end.

Yet he went on to produce some of the best bowling of his career. A little of the speed had gone by now, but he bowled with a minimum of wastage and, in green conditions, a maximum of movement. His Essex team-mates were convinced he was still good enough to play for his country.

He first played for Essex in 1967 and won his cap in 1970; by the late seventies, he was twice taking 100 wickets in a season. There had been an exciting Test debut for him at Delhi, where he took 7–46 against India.

His best figures to date came at Bristol in 1984, when Gloucestershire were hustled out sheepishly for 90 in the second innings and Lever, in just over 23 overs, took 8–37. Three of his wickets went for no runs in nine balls, and he did it with some notable swing. The hapless Gloucestershire batsmen returned to the middle for some extra practice as the bowler headed back to Chelmsford for the next fixture. He was proud of those figures but probably, in the way of most bowlers, no more than of his 91 runs against Glamorgan at Cardiff.

John Lever's easy, rhythmical action is one of the most attractive and effective in the game today. He swings the ball both ways and keeps the pressure on the batsman with his relentless accuracy.

Left-arm Pace

Left-arm pace – or left-arm swing bowling as I prefer to call it – is one of the most important arts within the game, and a good left-arm quick bowler is a valuable asset to any side. Spearing the ball in at batsmen from a different angle, a left-armer gives an orthodox attack complete variety and is a vital link in any bowling line-up. It's a variety which over the years has brought me a great deal of success and many wickets.

But I have had to work hard for my success. Being a left-armer and an opening bowler as well, it is my job to get the batsmen guessing from the outset. And the best time to strike is when the ball is new! Pitch it in the right place and the bowler can do almost anything when the ball is still hard and shiny and conditions are favourable.

But that's also when he has to be prepared to work his hardest.

Anybody can run up and swing the ball. But the art of swing bowling is setting it on the right line and forcing the batsman to play every delivery. Accuracy is crucial. Every over I bowl I aim to pitch the ball up, directing six out of six bang on the spot – five swinging away and the other swinging in.

With that aim in mind, bowling line and length on the off stump can pay handsome dividends. If the batsmen don't spot the inswinger they are almost certain to be out, either bowled or lbw.

Any decent left-armer should be able to swing the ball into the bat. In fact his stock ball has got to be the inswinger. But it was the one ball I couldn't bowl when starting out in cricket. I had to change my action to bowl the inswinger, and that meant working very hard at getting the action right.

All I wanted to be was a fast bowler, but at the age of twenty I realised I was never going to have the pace to develop into a real quickie. That's when I decided to concentrate on swing. I was lucky enough to be playing when the great Sir Gary Sobers was still going strong on the Test and county scene. Sobers could do almost anything with either bat or ball, and is without doubt the best exponent of left-arm swing bowling I have ever seen. He was the perfect model for any budding cricketer to watch.

Having a silky smooth action like Sobers is so important to any up and coming young bowler trying to make the grade. I spent hours hoping to pick up useful tips watching him and bowlers like Wesley Hall, Freddie Trueman and Dennis Lillee in full flight. Lillee's well-oiled run-up and delivery has been hailed as a classic and Hall's magnificent flowing action was truly a sight worth paying a lot of money to see. With actions like theirs a bowler is more likely to remain injury free, and fitness is an important factor for anyone striving to become a professional cricketer.

Although equally successful, Mike Proctor and Colin Croft were two strike bowlers with unconventional actions. They both suffered a few injuries, but generally adapted to their task very well.

Of our modern-day seamers Norman Cowans has a smooth action and, although very quick, sees himself more as a swing bowler. Kent's Richard Ellison, on the other hand, is a fine swing bowler although boasting no great pace. He operates from close to the stumps, which means he has less to do with the ball when he delivers it. My own bowling action is also looked upon very favourably in first-class cricket circles and it's mainly due to endless practice, fitness and remaining injury free.

Fitness is the key to success for the majority of pace bowlers. After all, a bowler is not much good to his captain if he can't be called upon to bowl at least twenty overs in a day. But there is a very fine line in keeping fit, and without doubt the best exercise for bowlers is bowling.

If a bowler feels comfortable with his action it is half the battle won, and the best advice I can give is . . . *look after your feet*. Well-fitting boots are essential. They will protect the ankles, which in turn look after the knees and so on up through the back muscles. We don't suffer too much on the softer grounds in this country, but it can be particularly tough going on rock-hard surfaces abroad where the knees come in for quite a pasting and the body in general suffers a severe battering.

But one thing all bowlers should remember, especially swing bowlers: the ball is the tool of your trade and should be carefully looked after. I think of it as an egg and treat it accordingly.

Gary Sobers was one of the finest left-arm fast-medium bowlers of his generation. Bowling over the wicket, he could make the ball swing late in either direction, concentrating his attack on or around the off stump.

It should be every bowler's ambition to get the most out of his bowling, and if he hopes to get wickets the ball must do what he wants it to do. So firstly, throughout a match, make sure it is kept in the best possible condition. Even though the ball might feel and look like a lump of old suede when it is several overs old, constant polishing on one side of the seam will make it deviate.

If the bowler's grip is right the ball should swing. How much depends on the ball and the conditions that prevail at the time. Cloud cover and a humid atmosphere provide the best climate.

It is then up to the bowler to exploit it by using all his skill and experience.

Speed, or lack of it, is very important. Some days, although conditions are perfect, a ball will do nothing. The bowler then has to adjust his tactics to achieve results. I've known days when the ball has gone straight through to the wicket-keeper when propelled at 100mph, only to swing all over the place following a subtle drop in pace.

But that can only happen by sheer luck or through years of hard-earned experience pounding up to the stumps.

Outswinger

1 Hold the ball with the first and second fingers alongside the seam; the thumb underneath, the third and fourth fingers supporting. The wrist is cocked backwards to begin with but straightens just before delivery. The weight goes on to the right leg as the shoulders open up.

2 At the moment of release the hand turns the ball towards first slip position. The ball is delivered with the hand upright.

3 The body falls away towards the on side as the ball is released. The left hand continues its turn in the follow-through; the left side comes right around. The right arm swings past and behind the right side, pulling the bowler away from the playing area.

Do's and Don'ts

Do's

1 The ball is your tool of the trade – look after it.
2 Use the correct grip and bowl the right line and length.
3 Use the conditions to the best advantage.
4 Train regularly and keep in peak fitness.
5 Work hard at all aspects of your game, especially at improving your action.
6 Wear the correct equipment.

Don'ts

1 Don't forget to practise regularly – practice makes perfect.
2 Don't be out-manoeuvred by the batsmen. Force them to play the strokes you want them to play and don't let them dictate the pattern of the game to you.
3 Don't give up when the chips are down. You have the answer to everything in your hands.

Inswinger

1 Hold the ball with the first and second fingers alongside the seam, the wrist cocked, the seam pointing in the direction of leg slip. The thumb is underneath, with the third and fourth fingers supporting.

2 Just prior to the moment of release. The weight is on the right leg. The shoulders open up. The hand straightens behind the ball.

3 The complete follow-through. The bowling arm swings out in front of the body in a long arc, keeping the seam in position. The weight goes over the right leg, the shoulders do a full turn.

MEDIUM PACE: ALEC BEDSER

Alec Bedser

Here was, and still is, a big man: big shoulders, big heart, big feet. Cobblers may have profited. Not so, one imagines, groundsmen who repaired the turf from his pounding. And not so batsmen, as they vainly tried to counter his late manifestations of seam, swing and 'straightening-out'.

Along with twin Eric, he joined Surrey shortly before the last world war. He *worked* at cricket because the working-class preoccupation of industry dominated his sub-conscious. By 1946 he was a Test bowler against India, and took 11 wickets in each of his first two matches. In all he took 1,924 wickets, 236 of them in his fifty-one appearances for England.

Alec Bedser was a medium-paced bowler of perfect action and wicked movement. He was an integral part of England's various post-war series against the Australians. The eyes under those deep green caps carried considerable respect and often unease. His battles with Bradman were engrossing, part of the game's history. Not many bowlers found a way to penetrate The Don's solid armour. Bedser did – and he still cherishes the elation of those occasions.

There was one marvellous performance by the Surrey seamer at Trent Bridge during the 1953 series. He ended up with 14 for 99, and that remained his best. The pace could be more than medium but the control was never for a moment sacrificed. He could cut the ball quite magnificently from leg.

Eleven times he took more than 100 wickets in a season. He may have been uncomplicated as a person but he could introduce disconcerting subtleties into his bowling. Today he remains self-contained, no-nonsense, pragmatic. He was first appointed an England selector in 1962 and from 1969–81 was chairman of the selection committee.

Alec Bedser bowled off an economically short run, with a perfectly balanced action that enabled him to avoid physical stress and strain. Fast medium, his stock ball was the inswinger moving very late in flight; he also bowled a slightly slower leg-cutter which was virtually unplayable on rain-affected pitches.
(TPS/Central Press)

Mike Hendrick, a magnificent fast-medium bowler with a model action whose career was sadly dogged by injury. The picture shows the effort that went into his delivery, the whippy arm action and full follow-through.

Medium Pace

The term medium-pace bowling covers a wide spectrum from the fast-medium type of bowler, which is just below genuinely fast, to the slow-medium type, which is just above slow bowling in pace. I will deal basically with fast-medium bowling, as to my mind that is the only bowler of this type to be really successful in Test matches.

Medium-pace to slow-medium bowlers are effective in county cricket and are now commonly called 'seam bowlers'. This term is used to describe the bowler of medium pace or below who endeavours to make use of the seam on the ball in order to make it deviate after pitching. This bowler has developed more in England because of the character of the pitches, coupled with the fact that nowadays the seam on the ball is more pronounced than it was. If the ball is pitched on the seam it will at times deviate, one way or the other, with the bowler often not knowing which direction it will take.

More and more bowlers of this type have developed since the introduction of limited-overs cricket. Basically they are used to restrict the batsman scoring. In Test cricket bowlers of medium pace relying solely on the use of the seam have proved to be generally ineffective, particularly overseas where Test pitches are harder with less grass. In order to make the ball move, more has to be done than just holding the seam up and hoping something will happen when the ball pitches. On the drier and firmer pitches abroad nothing much does happen unless the ball is actually spun.

For a fast-medium bowler to be an attacking bowler, he must be tall enough to be able to 'hit the ball into the pitch' at a full length in order to make it bounce. To be effective a bowler must:
1 Have or develop a good action.
2 Have command of length and direction.
3 Run up in a rhythmical, balanced and controlled manner, with not too long a run.
4 Have variety and change of pace.
5 Use the crease.
6 Be able to swing the ball late in its flight.

Max Walker, one of Australia's main strike bowlers in the '70s. Despite a somewhat awkward action, he was a highly effective bowler with the ability to cut the ball sharply away from the batsman.

A good action must be developed at an early age as it is very difficult to change one's action effectively once it has been moulded. To have a good natural action is obviously ideal. A good action is for the bowler to be in a sideways position, looking at the batsman over the bowler's left shoulder at the time of delivery. (Right-arm bowler – the reverse applies to the left-hander.) Emphasis is always placed on the position of the left shoulder, which is important. But I maintain the left hip must also be facing the batsman at the point of delivery. On delivery the hips should make a full turn so that the bowler's right hip finishes facing the batsman. (Right-arm bowler.) It is essential that the bowler should be able, when he arrives at the crease to deliver the ball, to rock back and propel himself on to a braced left leg (right-hand bowler), and remain as high as possible at the point of delivery. A good powerful follow-through is of the utmost importance – something which cannot be said too often.

For a fast-medium bowler to be effective in the highest grade of cricket he must be able to swing the ball late in its flight, whether it be into the batsman or away from him. I'm convinced that the ability to do this comes from a good strong body action and the use of the wrist. Unless the approach is rhythmical and unhurried, I don't think it is possible to complete a good body action.

Late swing is natural and is obvious at an early age. In my view, anyone who has this ability should develop his natural talent and not try to change, otherwise this invaluable asset could be ruined. I'm a great believer in developing one's natural ability.

It is essential that a fast-medium bowler should have command of length and direction; a real fast bowler can get away with erratic deliveries, even at the highest level, but not the fast-medium or medium-paced bowler. Accordingly much practice and hard work must be undertaken in order that the bowler can bowl a full length consistently. I emphasise a full length as too many bowlers bowl far too short; the definition of a good length is when a batsman is undecided whether he should play forward or back.

The simple way to practise this is to place a sheet of newspaper on the pitch, on the estimated good length position, and spend hours bowling at it. This type of practice can be done on any piece of ground – a perfect pitch isn't necessary – and I preferred to do it without the batsman at the crease. Once command of length has been obtained the bowler can then practise change of pace, and also the use of the return crease.

A modern term used is the bowling of a 'cutter' – that is, when a fast-medium or medium-pace bowler makes the ball deviate after hitting the pitch. Today many deliveries are so described when in fact all that has happened is that the ball has carried on its flight after it has swung, or has deviated because the large seam has caused it to move after hitting the pitch. The term cutter comes from the act of the bowler passing his fingers over the top of the ball when delivering it,

and in effect 'cutting' across the seam. What happens is that by this action the ball has had a certain amount of spin imparted at the time of release.

How effective a bowler can be when trying to bowl a cutter depends on his action and, more important, how strong his fingers are. It is essential with this type of delivery that the ball is bowled at a very full length. The ball can be cut either from leg to off or vice versa.

After a lot of practice I was able to make the ball move from leg to off after pitching, which in modern parlance is called the 'leg cutter' – but in fact I actually spun the ball and often held it in a similar manner to a leg-break bowler, delivering it

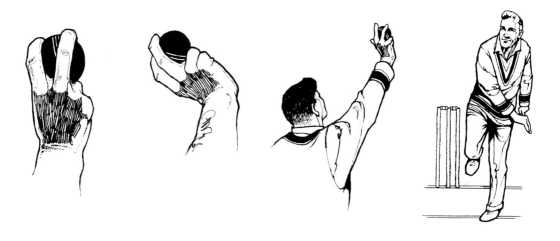

Leg Cutter

1 Place the ball in the right hand with the first and second fingers apart, and the inside of the second finger against the seam.

2 Turn the wrist to this position. To produce the cut, pull the second finger against the seam and push down the side of the ball with the first finger.

3 The moment before the release of the ball. The wrist is cocked backwards. The ball will be cut by the movement of the first two fingers across the seam from right to left.

4 The complete follow-through. The weight is over the left leg. The bent right leg steps over the front foot. The right hand continues the turn from right to left. The head is steady. The eyes follow the ball down the pitch.

with a bent wrist. At the end of the season I would have corns on my second and third fingers, which was proof that the ball was spun. I was fortunate enough to have big hands and strong fingers, which obviously helps.

A great deal of thought must be given when bowling, as so much depends on each individual thinking for himself. There is a tendency today for everyone to wait until they are 'coached' as to what to do.

I believe in players remembering what they can do naturally and then developing it. Too often people are told to change their action and to try and bowl like someone else, instead of bowling their own way. Someone who fully understands bowling can obviously see a fault in a bowler and in a matter of a few words can say what is wrong and what should be done to correct the error. It must be remembered, however, that although it may take five minutes to instruct, it can take months to eliminate the fault. There is no substitute for hard work.

When he has control of length and direction, the bowler can then study the batsman and devise a strategy to get him out. Not even the best of plans will necessarily work at once, but the bowler has far more chance of success if he has *control*. Which is where all that hard work and practice come in.

Off Cutter

1   Place the ball in the right hand with the first and second fingers close together and across the seam, with the inside of the second finger resting against the seam. The thumb and third finger support underneath; the little finger rests against the third finger.

2   About to deliver the ball. The first two fingers are in position to cut down and across the seam from left to right.

3   Seen from the back. The trunk has turned with the swing of the bowling arm and the hand cutting across the seam. The weight of the body is on the front leg.

4   The beginning of the follow-through with the hand turning after cutting across the ball from left to right, the trunk carrying on its turn. The right arm swings in front of the right side of the body.

OFF SPIN: JIM LAKER

Jim Laker

He wasted neither words nor emotions. As a television commentator, his views were laconic and one-toned. Away from the microphone, he was a fine raconteur, dry and rather acid, as you'd expect, and very funny. He didn't laugh a lot when he was bowling. But he was prepared to bowl nearly all day for Surrey.

Some would argue that there was never a better off-spinner. The evidence – if not the recognition – would seem to substantiate it. He took almost 2,000 wickets at 18.40. He joined Surrey in 1946 and left Essex in 1964. And yet, despite his considerable talents of spin and flight, he played in only forty-six Tests.

There was nothing automatic about his bowling. He was a man of variety and cunning, even deviousness. His action was high and relaxed. His expression could be interpreted as one of phlegm and, it seemed sometimes, more than a hint of cynicism. He had, some would say, a few valid reasons to feel cynical with those in authority.

Jim Laker started out a Yorkshireman with perhaps a career in banking. He was rather proud of his batting in the Bradford League. After the war his work briefly took him to London before Surrey beckoned. By 1947 he was being eased into the county side – and after only fourteen championship matches, he was selected for the West Indies tour. Half the party ended up injured or unfit. He ignored his own strains and took more wickets than anyone else.

The Australians tried to savage and destroy him. He saved up his retribution for 1956. Playing for Surrey against the Tourists, he took 10 for 88. A few weeks later, this slightly lugubrious six-footer took his historic 10 for 53 in the first innings and 9 for 37 in the second, this time in the Old Trafford Test. Laker could be unplayable like few other slow bowlers. They still talk at Bradford of his 8 for 2 in a Test trial.

Jim Laker died in April 1986, shortly before the book went to press. He will be remembered as long as the game of cricket is played.

Fred Titmus delivering his off-breaks under the watchful eye of former Somerset all-rounder Bill Alley. Titmus was particularly skilled at bowling the 'arm' ball – the one that drifts away from the right-hander.

Arguably the finest off-spinner ever, Jim Laker had a high sideways-on action, strong fingers that produced sharp spin, and an immaculate control of flight, length and pace. His extraordinary feat of taking 19 wickets in a Test against Australia is unlikely ever to be surpassed.
(TPS/Central Press)

Off Spin

I never bowled a serious off-spinner in my life until I had passed my twenty-first birthday. Fred Titmus and Ray Illingworth both started life as medium-paced bowlers. Tom Goddard of Gloucestershire, one of the greatest off-spinners I ever saw, began a distinguished career on the Lord's ground staff as a fast bowler. On the other hand both Lance Gibbs and Pat Pocock began spinning at an early age, all of which seems to prove that there is no set pattern for establishing a career as a first-class off-spin bowler.

There are of course many different types of off-spinners, varying from the medium-paced bowlers relying on cut rather than spin through to the slow and genuine spinner dependent on the amount of turn he can extract, coupled with variations of pace and flight. Yet they all must have a command of length and line.

Ideally the build of such a bowler should be around the six-foot mark. Very tall men are at a disadvantage in that it becomes quite difficult to attempt to flight the ball without overpitching – one finds as a result they become much too mechanical. Small men do have the advantage in that respect, yet in turn they have problems in finding that extra bounce from the pitch which can be of great value.

Of prime importance is the run-up and the bowling action itself. Too many people believe that the slow bowler need only take a couple of paces, and that he can do without the sideways-on action acknowledged as necessary for faster bowlers. A run-up of six or seven paces is ideal. With such an approach it is possible to introduce some variation, and it gives the bowler a better chance to use the crease – ie delivering the ball from both close to the wicket and from towards the end of the return crease. This varies the angle of flight towards the batsman.

Nowadays there appears to be a set pattern for the off-spinner, who will always bowl over the wicket to the right-handed batsman and only bowl round the wicket to the left-hander. Presumably this has come about because of the modern emphasis on limited-overs cricket. Obviously it is easier to fire the ball at a quicker pace towards the batsmen's legs by adopting this policy. Although I'm sure this makes good sense, particularly in one-day cricket, I still believe that in the first-class game the off-spinner is not complete until he can bowl accurately and at will from either side of the wicket, to all types of batsmen. A strong right-handed on-side batsman must favour the bowler coming over the wicket, yet may find more problems if he is forced to play against the changing angle of flight.

On good batting pitches it is a question of thinking every ball. Changes of pace must be subtle rather than obvious, use of the crease and variations of flight must come into play, yet all this is useless if length and line are not the prime factors. On the other hand, on a pitch which is taking some spin, these variations become less important and concentration on a combination of spin and accuracy becomes vital.

The art of controlling the spin also comes into the reckoning, and this, together with the 'arm' ball, is the most difficult thing to master. Long, strong fingers are essential for the big spinner, and it is the forefinger on which the strain is the greatest. To achieve maximum spin the first two fingers should grip the ball tightly across the seam, as wide apart as is physically possible. When the ball is released the forefinger should snap down towards the second finger, with the third and fourth fingers merely resting on the ball until the moment of release. Remember, too, that it is the top joints and almost the tips of the fingers which control the spin, and avoid having too much of the ball in the palm of the hand. If this happens, then you are rolling the ball out as opposed to spinning it.

To bowl off-spinners regularly and genuinely spin the ball must inevitably cause a good deal of soreness, and eventually a thickening of the forefinger joints. Examine the hands of professional off-spinners like Pat Pocock, Lance Gibbs or Ray Illingworth and you will see exactly what I mean.

As I have already mentioned, to vary and control the spin is none too easy. The grip described above is the one recommended for maximum turn. To reduce the purchase on the ball, place the forefinger not across the seam but alongside it, narrow the gap between the first two fingers, and cradle the ball towards the palm of the hand. The action of release must be the same as before, for

Lance Gibbs whose long fingers and high arm action enabled him to get exceptional spin and bounce.

Pat Pocock, an outstanding off-spinner who has been Surrey's principal spinning arm for more than twenty years.

any obvious change of action would immediately become apparent to an observant batsman.

One hears a great deal of talk about the 'arm' ball. It really means the ball bowled by the off-spinner which drifts away through the air towards the slips when bowled to a right-handed batsman. This particular delivery brought me a fair percentage of victims, usually caught either by the wicket-keeper or first slip with the batsman playing for the non-existent turn. I certainly could never bowl it at will, nor do I believe that anyone else can do so.

Once again my grip had to be varied. This I did without gripping the seam in any way, but rather by sliding the fingers across the shiny side of the ball. But equally important is to develop the perfect sideways-on action and deliver the ball from as close to the wicket as possible. Anyone with an open-chest action would find it almost impossible. For example, it was just about the one chink in the armour of that great West Indian, Lance Gibbs. Without any question Fred Titmus used the arm ball to greatest effect, with the South African Hugh Tayfield and Ray Illingworth also both accomplished artists.

To succeed at any level demands a good temperament, lots of concentration and constant practice. Every slow bowler, however good he may be, will come in for his share of punishment. No-one enjoys being hit out of the ground, but whenever that happens just take your time, concentrate and think harder next ball up. Correctly organised net practice is essential – and remember, you are better advised to spend forty-five minutes on serious and concentrated bowling than to wheel away for an hour and a half without giving each ball your full attention.

3 Just before the moment of release. The fore-finger is about to 'snap down' towards the second finger, left to right.

4 The complete follow-through. The weight is on and over the front leg, but with very little loss of height. The right knee is well forward. The hip has completed its quick turn. The hand stays in position after imparting the spin, and the arm has come across the body. The eyes watch the ball in the air going down the pitch.

Off Spin
1 Place the ball in the right hand and spread the first two fingers, as wide apart as possible, over the seam. The ball rests against the inside of the thumb and third finger.

2 From the front. The fingers are spread, the forefinger curled and ready to impart spin.

LEG SPIN: BILL O'REILLY

Bill O'Reilly

They called him 'Tiger'. He had no noticeable affection for batsmen and could turn a phrase as sharply as a leg-spinner. Bill O'Reilly was well over six foot, sparse of hair and, during the match, compliments. But he was, by the standards of any era, a great character – and a superb spin bowler.

Big Bill played for New South Wales from 1927 till just after the last world war. He made twenty-seven Test appearances for Australia and took 144 wickets. Greybeards contend that the successive balls with which he dismissed Joe Hardstaff and Wally Hammond in the 1938 Test at Leeds were unplayable. And he was in a paddy at the time, having just been no-balled!

His run-up and delivery were perhaps not of the kind that shuttered sportsmasters urged their pupils to copy. There was too much flailing of the arms, too much supposed stoop. But Bill never bothered his head too much with the niceties of orthodoxy. He bowled virtually at medium-pace, varied the leg-breaks with the googlies and the top-spinners. His accuracy was a by-word. So was his stamina.

He was the son of a schoolmaster and was a teacher himself for some years. And he was always a thinker. Every delivery was plotted; no spinner fired away at the leg stump with greater cunning and menace. He really established himself at Test level for the 'bodyline' series in 1932–3; he took 27 wickets, ten of them at Melbourne.

Quite apart from the prodigious spin that he imparted and the speed with which the ball arrived at the crease to disconcert a wary batsman, Bill complemented his shuffled skills with the ability to get regular and at times considerable bounce. With O'Reilly at one end and Clarrie Grimmett at the other, Australia paraded the sheer artistry of leg-break bowling like arguably never before or since.

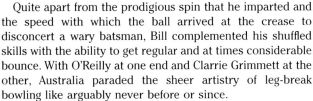

At a time when there was no shortage of good leg-spinners, Bill O'Reilly was one of the greats. He bowled at almost medium pace, had a devastating and well-concealed googly, and used his height to achieve considerable bounce. Unlike most leg-spinners, he maintained remarkable accuracy and control.
(TPS/Central Press)

Leg-spinner Bob Holland whose five wickets in England's second innings at Lord's in 1985 were the decisive factor in Australia's victory.

70

Leg Spin

If I were a lucky young boy, uncommonly keen on playing cricket and possessing an Aladdin's Lamp, I should immediately decide that I wished to become a highly competent leg-spin bowler bound for the international arena.

Batsman – no fear! That's far too uninteresting. Something that really makes you think, if you please, my dear Aladdin, because I am certain that the present international stage is just waiting for a tough leg-spinner to drop in and play incredible havoc.

The best leg-spinner that has lived this 'mortal coil', so far, was Clarence Victor Grimmett, a magnificent present given Australia by the New Zealand city of Dunedin back in 1912 when he migrated to my country. Ambitious young cricketers keen to cash in on the present dearth of leg-spinners in England, Australia and the West Indies could find nothing more fundamentally valuable than to make a close study of the Grimmett story from 1912 to 1930 and beyond, when he was the outstanding bowler in the world and had won a series for Australia in England almost entirely alone. That was in 1930.

Don Bradman helped! He scored 974 Test runs at an average of 139.14 that year, thereby introducing the theme of immortality and convincing all England that it would certainly be no fluke if he were to finish his whole Test career with an average of 99 per innings – which he did.

But Grimmett's 29 wickets from 349 overs at an average of 32 (and under three runs an over; an impressively low figure for a leg-spinner) took precedence, in my humble opinion, over the Don's incredible performance as an Ashes-winning contribution on that tour. Bradman was backed up by four batsmen who each averaged over 50 runs per innings and two more who managed 35 or over. Grimmett had no spin support at all. He was called upon to bowl more than sixty overs per Test and dealt with batsmen like Jack Hobbs, Walter Hammond, Herbert Sutcliffe, Prince Duleepsinhji, Maurice Leyland, Frank Woolley and Percy Chapman – an array custom-built to put the fear of the Lord into the heart of any leg-spinner, bar the world's best.

Clarrie never adhered to the fallacious theory that leg-spinners must 'loop' the ball, a custom, so it seems, now a basic law with all modern coaches and critics. For him looping was for the

Pakistan's Abdul Qadir, one of the few leg-break and googly bowlers of world class to have emerged in recent years. His naturally aggressive instinct is reflected in his brisk arm action and energetic follow-through.

73

birds. Bowling to batsmen of Test calibre, Clarrie would 'push the ball through' onto the blind spot with the idea of keeping his batsman-victim pinned to back-foot defence.

Playing the 'cat and mouse' game with a man like Hammond, who was perhaps the best off-side driver to have appeared in Tests in Grimmett's time, the little leg-spinner knew that survival for the slow bowler meant nothing more than lulling the batsman to sleep on his back foot.

Unlike most spinners Grimmett considered it unprofitable to spin a long way. The dividend was not attractive enough. Unlike, in particular, the other highly successful Australian leg-spinner, Arthur Mailey, who was the doyen of his kind in the early twenties after the Great War and who went for spin in a big way. His leg-break fairly 'sang' in mid-air as it wobbled in against the breeze, and his 'wrong 'un' or googly (or 'Bosey' as it was known then in Australia) could turn a foot.

That gifted spinner with all of his emphasis on spin was often guilty of frailty both in length and direction. His enormous 'turn' was quite impossible to maintain without revealing almost inexcusable errors in length and direction, a weakness also peculiar to another great Australian spinner, Fleetwood-Smith, later on.

I once saw Mailey clean bowl Victorian right-hander Les Keating on the second bounce in Sydney, and all the interested world knows that he once bowled the great Jack Hobbs with a slow full toss.

Indeed Mailey used to openly state in his columns (he was a journalist) that his consistent inaccuracy was the most helpful feature of his spin attack. Once he criticised me in Sydney during the first 'bodyline' Test for bowling far too mechanically. There was no future for me handling leg-breaks and 'wrong 'uns' in the way I did, as though I were a bowling Scrooge.

Grimmett had no time whatever for weaknesses in either length or direction, and this attitude of his, together with his insistence upon grooving himself to reduce his spinning to his own idea of the irreducible minimum, made him the most valuable leg-spinner ever to set foot on an Anglo-Australian Test field.

Spinning, when all is said and done, is just a simple matter.

Take the ball in your hand and toss it straight up in the air a yard or two, making it spin around in exactly the opposite direction from the hands of a clock, and catching it as it falls. To make the job easier, use a tennis ball – it is soft and you can dig your fingers into it. The quicker or more powerfully you use your fingers the harder the ball will revolve.

The 'right' grip for your leg-break is the one that gives you the best result as to the speed and comfort of the exercise. Never, I repeat never, go to a coach and ask to be shown the right grip to bowl a leg-break. You alone are the one who must discover what grip is right for you – so set about it straight away, just as soon as you can lay your hands on a tennis ball.

The first time I was invited to attend the Sydney Cricket Ground nets as a twenty-year-old newcomer who had, as a country boy, taught himself how to bowl leg-breaks and 'wrong 'uns', I was absolutely 'flattened' when the great Arthur Mailey, then a spinning immortal, advised me to change my grip substantially. Indeed he went so far as to say that the grip I was using reminded him of the way he gripped his number five iron.

Courteously, I think, I thanked him for his suggestion, but left little doubt in his mind that I intended to carry on with it and to sink or swim still holding the ball the same way as I had taught myself ten years before.

Suddenly an old man wearing an overcoat and a bowler hat came up to me at the spectator end of the nets and said, 'I heard all that, Mr O'Reilly, and I wish to congratulate you on your self-confidence. Exactly the same thing happened to me when I came down from the bush forty-five years ago.'

It was Charles Turner – 'Turner the Terror' who carried Australia on his bowling back in the 1880s and early '90s with his slow off-spinners. I was so completely flabbergasted by the kindly old man's intervention that it didn't even occur to me that here was an opportunity to get one of the most prized autographs ever.

Once you have your own 'right' grip and have recognised the strength of spin you start on the most important job of all – teaching yourself the real meaning of length.

Length, strangely enough, is quite intangible. Spin and direction are easy. You can see for yourself what you are doing – right or wrong – in that regard, but length is something that can

change significantly for each batsman who faces you.

A good length to a midget who could ride the lightweight in the Melbourne Cup would certainly not be the one you would bowl to his partner who could qualify physically for the heavyweight boxing championship of the British Isles – Lindsay Hassett and Greg Chappell, so to speak.

The real conception of the appropriate length becomes ingrained only after long and concentrated practice.

I know that for many people thinking is something to be avoided with the utmost possible speed. It hurts far too much. But I warn you that if you are not prepared to think about length every time you take ball in hand, then it would be far better for you to stay at home and feed the chooks.

A batsman facing up to a leg-spinner must decide instantaneously, as soon as the ball is launched, whether he is going to play forward or back to deal with it safely. That is his problem.

The spinner's problem is to make him pull the wrong rein – that is, to trick him into playing forward to one which really requires back-foot

Richie Benaud bowling for NSW against the MCC at Sydney in 1958. Benaud's repertoire included the leg-break, googly, top-spinner (the ball which gains pace off the wicket but doesn't turn), and the 'flipper' – flipped out of the hand from underneath the wrist and in effect an off-spinning top-spinner.
(TPS/Central Press)

defence. That means that, fundamentally, most of a spinner's subtleties – the most destructive by far in a batsman's opinion – come into play before the spinning ball even hits the pitch.

As you develop your stock-in-trade you will proudly gloat over the trivial terms used by the cricket writers to describe the tricks which you have profitably brought into play. The funniest of these I think is 'dropped'. For instance: 'Playing forward confidently to O'Reilly, Woolley was easily caught by McCabe at short mid-wicket when the ball appeared to "drop" and bounce high.'

No bowling magician could possibly do that; it just cannot happen. All that did happen was that Frank failed to pick the slow 'wrong 'un' and arrived far too early at his proposed point of contact.

This example took place in the Oval Test in 1934, when the brilliant left-handed hitter from Kent, who had never faced me before, was chosen for the final match of the series for the sole purpose of belting me out of the attack. A few days later I learned on meeting Frank somewhere along the Strand that no-one had taken the trouble to inform him that I had a 'wrong 'un' in my quiver.

Thinking is so vitally important for a leg-spinner that he must actually set out right from the start to be his own severest critic. Every ball he bowls – at the nets or in the middle – must be summed up critically and carefully in his own mind.

Remember that spinning is, as I have said before, a very simple job, but the salesmanship required to make it a highly essential Test-cricket commodity is the whole crux of the trade. That indeed is where the thinking comes in.

The silly idea that English wickets are not for leg-spinners should be thrown right out of an English window. I myself collected 50 of my 102 Test wickets against England in England, and for more convincing evidence still I go back again to my champion partner Grimmett, who took 69 of his 106 Test aggregate on the so-called difficult pitches of the Old Country.

Leg-break

1 Hold the ball with the seam sideways on. Grip with the first three fingers. The third finger, bent and against the seam, imparts the spin.

2 The wrist is cocked, the palm upwards, the fingers spread. The right arm begins its upward swing, and the hand begins to turn.

3 The ball is about to be released. The hand comes over with the third finger imparting the spin. Because the hand is turning from right to left, the shoulder and trunk open up to assist the movement.

4 The right arm comes across the body with the right-to-left movement of the bowling hand; the body balance goes forward over the braced left leg.

Please, Mr Aladdin, give me use of your famous lamp.

How I would enjoy myself returning to the scene where every batsman around has learned to lunge forward as though by second nature. Again I advise every thoughtful youngster with cricket in his veins to get himself on the spin bandwagon and diligently prepare himself for immortality. Present-day batsmen are all, in my opinion, fit for the kill.

If the term 'wrong 'un' worries you, stop being concerned immediately. As you are flicking that tennis ball high above your head, experiment with moving your wrist around and note carefully what effect this has. Soon you will see that the same fingers which make the ball spin anti-clockwise will give entirely the opposite result if the wrist goes all the way round. Try it.

But prepare for trouble when you attempt to bowl it overarm. That's where the problem lies. It is a *very* difficult ball to master. It seems to defy all your rules, self-made, of length and direction. The bowler who can manage it, by dint of hours and hours, days and days, weeks and weeks and on to years of practice, can start preparing to deal with the autograph-hunters.

I hope, sincerely hope, that I am there to add weight to the cheering.

Googly

The googly, or 'wrong 'un', is an off-break bowled with a leg-break action, but with the wrist turning over earlier than for the leg-break.

1   The ball is held in a grip similar to that for the leg-break, with the wrist cocked. To begin with the hand is palm upwards, but as the bowling arm swings into the upright position the hand reverses itself so that it is facing the ground.

2   The ball is about to be released. The hand continues to roll over, the back of it now facing the batsman.

3   The hand turns over. The ball is 'flipped' out over the top of the third and fourth fingers, as the third finger imparts left-to-right spin. The chest is almost square-on. The dipping left shoulder assists the 'inside out' turn of the hand.

4   The hand turns completely 'inside out', with the inside of the forearm facing the batsman. The left shoulder goes up as the body weight moves over the front leg in the follow-through.

LEFT-ARM SPIN: DEREK UNDERWOOD

Derek Underwood

Derek Underwood plays the game with the minimum of fuss and personifies efficiency. He's a quiet man who hurries through his overs with a glint of ruthlessness in his eyes. His nickname is 'Deadly'; it symbolises the unwavering accuracy of his bowling.

He's faster than most left-arm spinners – and, it must be said, flatter. He cuts the ball; he contains the scoring. His critics would call him a defensive bowler, pledged to curb the aggressive flourishes of the batsman. He'd probably argue that he is a bowler who attacks and challenges his adversary to go after him.

His first season, 1963, was one of rare and extraordinary success. He proceeded to take 100 wickets, the youngest player to do so in his debut year. Wiseacres perked up, asked who he was and implied that he should change his style. He should slow down and try to spin the ball more. He didn't need such a long run-up. He listened courteously and from time to time experimented. Then he returned to his original and natural action.

The sensational opening season at the age of eighteen was no phoney statement from an upstart. He kept taking wickets – at his own pace, on his own terms. By 1966 he was playing for England. Two years later, at The Oval where as a boy he was taken to watch Lock and Laker, he finished with 7–50 to level the series against the Australians. By the age of twenty-five he had taken more than 1,000 first-class wickets.

'Deadly' played in eighty-six Tests and, as we all know, there could have been more. His temperament never let him down during a match. Now he's past forty and great batsmen continue to pay him the compliment of surveying that ten-pace run with as much respect and even apprehension as ever. He has an ageless merit that makes him an asset to any captain.

Bishan Bedi, one of the greatest left-arm spinners of all time. A master of flight and spin, he had a beautifully relaxed action which enabled him to bowl all day long without losing rhythm or control.

Although classified as a spinner, Derek Underwood cuts rather than spins the ball, relying on skilful variations of pace and angle to beat the bat. On wet pitches he can be almost unplayable, and his unflagging accuracy and control are an object lesson for any bowler.

Left-arm Spin

Yes, I know what you are going to say – I'm not quite your typical slow left-arm spinner. I am supposed to be more medium-paced than slow. Well, so were Hedley Verity, that tall and distinguished Yorkshireman, and Charlie Parker, Gloucestershire's pre-war rascal who took 3,278 wickets and yet played only once for his country.

There has been a good deal of advice given to me over the years. They said I bowled too fast and I bowled too 'flat'. They said my run-up was too long and that I didn't vary my deliveries sufficiently. I'd dispute a few of those points!

But, of course, advice is usually well-meaning. From the early days when I received some invaluable coaching from the likes of Ken Barrington and Tony Lock, at an indoor school at Croydon, I was desperately eager to learn. I listened intently to everything they told me. I may have been considered something of a *fast* bowler at school but I discovered the vast gulf between bowling at that and at adult level.

So my first piece of basic advice is *listen and learn*. One can never have too much practice. My father used to play village cricket in Kent and I went along to watch him – and bowl to my older brother alongside the pavilion. When we went to the seaside, probably to Westgate, I never failed to take my tennis ball. As the tide came in, so we moved up onto the top of the cliffs, where we used a hard ball.

This kind of *enthusiasm* is so important. At prep school, we had the choice of athletics or cricket on Wednesday afternoons. My great thrill was when one of the masters took me to The Oval to see Lock, Laker and Barrington. Those were great days for Surrey, of course – and for me. My appetite was whetted for ever.

The spin bowlers fascinated me. My eyes never strayed from Tony Lock and Jim Laker when they were wheeling away. Even as a schoolboy, I studied their techniques and envied their unerring accuracy. I noted the way Lock revised his technique and became without doubt the finest *attacking* slow left-arm bowler in the world. One of my first lessons had been absorbed – a slow bowler could also attack.

In my case, I'm categorized as a spin bowler. But I'm really a cutter. I come in off 10 yards and deliver a ball which at that speed cuts rather than spins. From the days when Tony Lock approached

Kent's Les Todd and I was given a trial for the county, the ability to cut the ball has come fairly natural to me. This is because of my particular wrist action – not unlike the turning of a door handle – a valuable bonus to me.

Let us take the case of the finger-spinner. In the early stages it isn't so important learning *how* to spin the ball. Your priority should be to acquire enough control to be able to bowl a length and line – so that you can land the ball exactly where you want it. There will be time later for refining your skills and learning to do things with the ball.

So the No 1 aim must be *length and line*. Accuracy, in other words. And that applies whether you are bowling for your village third eleven or your county side.

Where should you pitch the ball? That obviously depends on many things – the state of the wicket, whether it's turning or how much it is turning.

Let's assume the wicket isn't turning. As a general rule, the left-arm spinner should aim to pitch just outside off stump so that the ball drifts in towards middle-and-off. But if the wicket is taking spin, then you'd probably try to pitch more on the leg-stump line. That would make the batsman play and commit himself.

We have all seen bowlers – slow ones as well as the quickies – run into technical problems. It's a sad and embarrassing spectacle and fellow players have a great sympathy for those who are suffering. Suddenly, for all sorts of complicated and mental reasons, they have trouble with their grip, their run-up and their overall control.

The orthodox grip for the slow left-arm bowler is often likened to that of the right-arm off-spinner – with everything in reverse. In other words, the left-arm bowler's fingers turn in an anti-clockwise direction.

Run-up? It's surprising how many young slow bowlers have difficulty making up their minds here. Do what is right for you to acquire the ideal rhythm. *Poise and balance* are what you must aim for. You must feel right when you run in to bowl. Ten paces is right for me. I can get maximum rhythm in that way. I must be honest – I like to see a slow bowler with a distinct, easy run rather than the one who 'stands and bowls'.

There is no easy answer for the potential slow spinner who wants to know how much air he should give the ball. The first-class game is structured in such a way, of course, with the abundance of one-day matches, that the tendency is not to 'buy' wickets but to 'contain' the batsman. Therefore, the bowler is inclined to push the ball through. I remember how Tony Lock used to throw the ball up when he started. Experience taught him to cut back on the flight after that.

I come back again to the advice I was given. The result was that I experimented and tried to bowl slower, for instance. I remember that I went through a phase when it was suggested the umpire might stand back and I should run up between him and the wicket. In the end I resorted to *what was natural for me*.

That is something I recommend to slow left-arm bowlers. It reinforces the old saying that bowlers are born and not made. Having said that, there is still scope for him to build on his natural abilities.

A word or two now about variation. We have all read and heard tales about great bowlers who supposedly foxed the batsman by continually changing the kind of delivery offered to him. They say Cecil Parkin, the former Lancashire spinner, frequently paraded six different deliveries in an over. Maybe he did – but it isn't my style.

It's essential to establish your *stock delivery and the standard pace*. Now, if you wish, you can work on a few variations. But don't be too ambitious. There is a danger that if you try to be too clever, your range of bowling will become counter-productive and you may even lose your greatest natural assets.

In county cricket, few experienced players are going to be outwitted and even mildly troubled if I switch from a quick to a very slow delivery. It needs to be far more subtle. On the other hand, the one that is *slightly* quicker or slower than my stock delivery has a better chance of success.

I mentioned Charlie Parker earlier. He had this wonderful, intuitive relationship on the field with Wally Hammond, who crouched in the slips or gully and just kept taking the catches. The slow bowler relies a good deal on his fielders. That brings me to Alan Knott, with whom I have had a rare and vital rapport for years. 'Knotty' can be an inspiration, of course.

Phil Edmonds appears to be watching the ball in flight instead of focusing on where it should pitch. An intelligent and imaginative bowler, he prefers to take the attack to the batsman even if it means giving away runs in the process.

Sometimes I used to think he knew what I was going to bowl before I did! He's always nagging me to bowl quicker. Quicker, I ask you . . . I'm apt to say to him: 'Come off it, I'm forty now!'

The two of us would work on various theories. We perfected a leg-side stumping for left-handed batsmen and we would succeed three or four times a season – an extremely satisfactory outcome.

Field placings are important but they depend on the state of the game – whether the batsman is just in, whether he's well set. I advise aspiring young left-arm bowlers to build up understandings with their wicket-keepers (even if they aren't quite in the class of Knotty) and the close fielders.

I like to put a new batsman under immediate pressure and would suggest you do the same. That means bringing up the extra fielder for the bat-and-pad catch. Apart from perhaps a silly point, I might have my short leg, and bring up a gully and second slip. Nothing disconcerts a new batsman more than to have a cluster of four fielders all round him. They can be gradually removed as he becomes set and starts to build his score – unless we get him first!

According to the circumstances of the particular match, it is sometimes justified to try to 'buy' a wicket. I know slow bowlers who very

Left-arm Spin

1 Grip the ball with the first, second and third fingers apart, the thumb underneath, the first and second fingers across the seam.

2 The ball is spun with the first finger at the moment of release.

3 Just before the ball is delivered. The weight is over the right leg. The hand is in position, the wrist cocked back. The shoulders are opening up, the head is steady.

4 The delivery. The weight has gone over the right leg. Both arms are continuing their swing, the left arm cutting across the body. The left hand completes a full turn after spinning the ball.

consciously adopt a policy of feeding a batsman's strengths at the start of his innings. I can see the reasoning or apparent cunning in that. But I don't ever do that. My undeviating philosophy is to *avoid a batsman's strengths*, never do anything which is going to make life easier for him.

If I'm bowling to Geoff Boycott, the last thing I want to do is bowl him one short of a length outside his off stump, tailor-made for his favourite square cut. I like bowling to him – there is a mutual respect and the challenge is particularly satisfying. I'd like all young slow bowlers to look on every ball as a personal challenge.

It's partly a mental battle. As a slow bowler, you'll be expected to keep going for long spells. Perhaps there's no sign of a wicket coming and your performance deteriorates as you become increasingly anxious. In the process, you must somehow sustain the accuracy, avoiding the long-hops and full tosses.

So don't let a lean spell get you down and affect your concentration. Remember – length and line, rhythm, poise and balance . . . and an ability to plug away. Good luck!

The Chinaman
An off-break bowled by a left-hander with a leg-break action.

1 The grip with the first three fingers spread well apart.

2 The position of the hand just before the upward swing of the bowling arm. The ball is held in a similar fashion to the right-hand leg-break, and the spin will be imparted with the third finger.

3 About to release the ball. The hand is turning over in a rolling movement, the spin on the ball left to right.

4 The complete follow-through. The weight has gone on and over the right leg. The trunk and shoulders complete a full turn as the left arm swings across the body.

WICKET-KEEPING: BOB TAYLOR

Bob Taylor

Some would argue that he was a better wicket-keeper than Alan Knott. He was not as good a bat and that swayed the selectors. It meant he had to be patient, wondering if the Kent physical-jerker would ever start dropping his catches. Knott didn't – but he went off instead to play for Packer. And Taylor, the superb technician, was elevated to Test stature.

He was in the Keith Andrew mould: still, eagle-eyed, without ostentation. You suspected he didn't approve too much of wicket-keepers who had a propensity for swallow dives and basketball leaps. He was the model for all young, aspiring stumpers. There was never a snatch or a superfluous movement. He had an envied rapport with his bowlers. Well, almost all the time – not when Phil Edmonds dared to summon up pace and let go a couple of bouncers in the opening Test of the 1978–9 Australian series. Edmonds just didn't bother to let Taylor know. Communication was restored, and somewhat to the point, between Mike Brearley and the bowler at the end of the over.

Bob Taylor was much liked in the game. He had a pleasant, amiable manner and was known by everyone as 'Chat'. In some ways he tended to drift away from younger players whose attitudes were different from his. He was a traditionalist, from another mould, another era.

He made his debut in 1960 (one match) and didn't give up till 1984. His 1,646 dismissals during that marvellous span is a world record. In 1966 at Derby, he caught seven Glamorgan batsmen in an innings. So he did against Yorkshire at Chesterfield in 1975 – and for England, no less, against the Indians at Bombay four years later. His ten catches in that Bombay match created a world Test record.

An unassuming man, the compliments probably embarrassed him. In truth, his 100 – his only one – at Sheffield in 1981 no doubt gave him just as much private joy. Who's going to be ungenerous enough to suggest that the Yorkshire bowlers had an off day?

Bob Taylor, Derbyshire and England, world record-holder for the most dismissals in first-class cricket.

Alan Knott displays his customary agility and control as he collects a wide ball from Ray Illingworth and whips off the bails in the same movement. Batsman Roy Fredericks was adjudged not out and went on to score 150. England v West Indies at Edgbaston, 1973.

Wicket-keeping

They say that wicket-keepers are born, not made. I suppose it's true to a degree. To reach international level you must have natural ability, though that shouldn't deter any young wicket-keeper with more modest ambitions. If you practise hard at techniques, you can make yourself a very competent school or club 'keeper.

First of all though you have to want to do the job, and not be afraid of the hard ball! I wanted to keep wicket from a very early age, mainly because I was fed up with standing at third man or fine leg, not doing anything. I wanted to be among the action and to be involved in helping the team to success. I suppose every top sportsman has to be an extrovert or confident in his own ability.

During those early days of keeping wicket, I certainly didn't realise I had natural ability. This was brought out of me by my coach and mentor Jack Ikin, of Lancashire and England. He coached me sometimes four or five nights a week in the summer, and helped me in my progress through

each stage of my amateur career from schoolboy to club to Minor Counties cricket.

To be a successful wicket-keeper there are three main disciplines to follow:

Concentration You must expect every delivery to come through to you – ie that the batsman is going to miss the ball not play it. Concentration is obviously a question of mind over matter. Not even the best coach in the world can teach you how to concentrate; it's up to the individual. Train yourself to switch off from everything else when the ball is being bowled. This is a tough discipline, one that is difficult to master, but you can't become a good wicket-keeper without it.

Staying Down This means staying down in the normal crouched position as long as possible. Again it is timing in the mind. I always think that you can stay down until the ball has actually pitched, then start to raise your body with the arms hanging down in front of you, hands below knee level. This helps you to take the ball that doesn't rise. It is much easier to come up with the rising ball than to go down to one that keeps low.

Don't Snatch Give with the ball; don't go towards it but allow the ball to come to you.

I've mentioned the three main disciplines for keeping wicket. These apply of course whether you're standing up to the slow bowler or medium-pacer, or standing back to the fast bowler. Generally though it's standing up to the wicket that sorts out the good wicket-keeper from the 'stopper'!

Standing Up When standing up to a right-handed batsman the wicket-keeper should have his left foot in line with the middle-and-off stump, with his feet far enough apart to be comfortable. He should be in a crouched position, hands between the legs, with the fingers pointing down and resting on the ground just behind the back line. When taking a delivery outside the off stump, stay down until the ball pitches, then rise with it. After each take, go through the action of bringing the hands back to the stumps as if you are going to

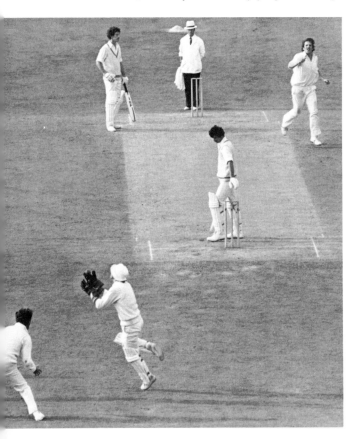

Richard Hadlee edges an away-swinger from Ian Botham and Bob Taylor, anticipating well, quickly makes ground to take the catch in front of Mike Brearley at first slip. A good wicket-keeper can 'widen the slips' by covering much of the first-slip position himself.

stump the batsman. This gets you into the habit, just in case the batsman decides to leave the crease and give the wicket-keeper a stumping chance.

The take down the leg side can be somewhat more difficult because you lose sight of the ball momentarily. As soon as the wicket-keeper picks the line of the ball going down the leg side, he must move across as fast as possible. The most

New Zealand wicket-keeper Ian Smith takes a spectacular diving catch to dismiss Bob Willis at Lord's in 1983. Smith has judged the catch well with the ball clearly falling short of Geoff Howarth at first slip.

effective way is to chassis or click the feet together, turning the left foot in towards the wicket. This keeps you close to the stumps, so that if the batsman leaves the crease you are able to whip off the bails. When moving across, keep your head and eyes as still as possible – if you move a camera you get a distorted picture; the same happens if you throw your head around. And don't forget to keep your arms dangling down in front of you with your hands below the level of your knees, for the one that keeps low.

Standing Back How far do you stand back? That depends on two things: first, the pace of the bowler; second, the pace of the wicket. In the first over of the innings the wicket-keeper should be catching the ball at about waist height. If you are taking the ball shoulder high you're too close, thus lessening your chances of catching a snick. If you are catching the ball around your ankles, then you're too far back and, again, if the batsman snicks the ball it won't carry to you.

General Hints The wicket-keeper is the king-pin of the fielding side as he gets most chances to dismiss batsmen. Always be lively, agile and encouraging. If you're all these things and accept chances that are given, then you will inspire the rest of the fielders. Remember that catches win matches. All the successful teams, at whatever level, have a superior all-round fielding side.

When standing back, try to get up to the wicket to receive throw-ins. Raise one arm in the air so that the fielder can judge better from the boundary where his target is. Always try to make bad throws into good ones.

Try and encourage the bowlers, particularly the pace bowlers. Sometimes they think the ball isn't getting down to the other end fast enough. Keep them going at the end of the over by giving them the impression that the ball is seaming, swinging and coming into your gloves hard. This gives them a boost and often results in their next delivery being bowled even faster.

Fitness The wicket-keeper has to be fitter than anyone else in the team. He's stretching up and bending down all the time, on the move up to the wicket after almost every delivery when standing back. I always think that if you're physically fit it must help your mental fitness as well, which enables you to concentrate for longer periods of time. Strong legs are essential and I would recommend lots of hill running and climbing – on soft ground, of course, to save any jarring of the knee joints. Groin and hamstring exercises are also essential to keep the body agile for those diving catches.

Wicket-keeping Practice Some players like to practise in the nets. Personally, I would only do it if there was adequate room behind the wicket and only two bowlers at any one time bowling at the batsman. If you get three or four different types of bowler in one net, the wicket-keeper hardly has time to compose himself and concentrate properly, in which case you achieve very little in the way of useful practice.

One good exercise to do to speed up your reactions, particularly during the winter months when you might be practising indoors, is to stand facing a blank wall, say two metres away, and get a colleague to throw a tennis ball at different angles from behind you, for you to catch the rebound off the wall. When you've practised this successfully, make it a little more difficult by turning round so that your back is to the wall and you are now facing your partner: when he throws the ball at the wall, you have to turn quickly in either direction to catch it.

One final thought: Always enjoy your cricket and wicket-keeping. And at the end of the day, if you've tried your best, no-one can argue with that.

1 Stance at the crease
Both knees are fully bent to adopt a sitting-down position. The right foot is outside the off stump. The head is steady. The chin is up. The eyes are looking past the batsman for the ball as it leaves the bowler's hand. The backs of the hand touch the ground with the palms facing forward.

2 Taking the good length delivery outside the off stump

The right foot has moved towards the off side. The 'keeper has stood up, bringing the hands to the height of the ball. The hands have remained with palms facing forward. The balance of the body is also slightly forward.

3 Taking the yorker well outside the off stump

From the original stance position, the right foot has slid out and back towards the off side along the ground, and the hands, also keeping their original stance position, go back. The eyes watch the ball as far as possible. From this position, the hands can take the ball back towards the stumps easily if a stumping chance arises.

4 Taking the ball outside the off stump and positioning the hands for a stumping chance

The balance of the body goes towards the right leg. The 'keeper stands up, bringing the hands to the height of the ball. The right hand, palm forward, is ready to take the ball. The left hand is in position to join up with the right hand when that hand sweeps towards the stumps.

5 Taking the ball outside the leg stump

The ball is about to be taken. The weight is on the left leg. The left elbow high, bringing the left hand up. The right shoulder dips as the right hand reaches across the body to join up with the left.

OUTFIELDING: DEREK RANDALL

Derek Randall

It was sometimes said that Derek Randall got into the Test side on the strength of his fielding. That was rubbish – but it still implied what a buoyant bonus he was to any bowling side as he prowled the covers or patrolled the outfield, ever ready to save the second run or deceive complacent batsmen by the lethal accuracy of his return.

He first played for Nottinghamshire in 1972 and for England, against Australia, in 1976. Since then he has exasperated and, more often, delighted. Many would argue that the selectors should have been less wary of his apparently idiosyncratic approach to batting. The trouble was that he never seemed able to keep still. He shuffled, he went on afternoon rambles between deliveries, and acquired a plethora of mannerisms that were apt to obscure his considerable batting skills.

Derek Randall is, at his best, a very fine batsman. His 174 in the Centenary Test at Melbourne in 1977 demonstrated that. But there have been many innings rich in positive stroke-making and canny technique that can too easily be forgotten amid the self-rebuking murmurs and the fidgets, which it must be said have lessened over the years.

He's impish and absent-minded. The outward manifestations of his ebullient and rather nervous disposition must never be stifled. That is part of his charm. The spectators chuckle at the way he plays his cricket; not so those Aussie bowlers renowned for a fiery nature and lack of good humour.

'Arkle', as he's known, is a natural athlete. That is why his timing at the crease is often so good. It's why he must remain a model for every young cricketer who wants to become a better fielder. He so clearly enjoys saving fours and stopping batsmen in their tracks. No-one takes a liberty when the ball goes to him.

Derek Randall runs out Sunil Gavaskar in typically brilliant fashion in the Edgbaston Test of 1979.
(Top) Randall moves quickly from mid-on, anticipating that Gavaskar's shot will beat Edmonds at short leg.
(Middle) His quick pick up and return finds Taylor at the wicket with Gavaskar yards out of his crease.
(Bottom) Brearley and Botham in the slips join in the appeal.

Outfielding

There is no doubt in my mind that my fielding got me into the Nottinghamshire team initially and the same is true of every other level of cricket at which I have played.

My first contact with the England team was as twelfth man for a Test at Trent Bridge against New Zealand when, by tradition, they pick on a local player who is likely to save a few runs if his services are required. I am equally sure my fielding was taken into consideration when I got my first England cap. It stands to reason that if you have a couple of young batsmen of about the same ability and one is a better fielder, he will get the vote.

Fielding – and fielding practice – is often regarded as the boring part of cricket. This is especially true at schoolboy level where it is seen as a means of filling in the time before a youngster gets his chance to bat or bowl. I can understand this, remembering only too well how difficult it was at times to work at improving my fielding when I might have been concentrating on the more glamorous aspects of the game.

It was not always easy, for example, disciplining myself to turn up at Trent Bridge in the middle of winter, stick one stump in the ground and spend the next couple of hours collecting a ball and trying to knock it over. That is what I mean about hard work but, I can assure you, it is worth doing in the long run.

I eventually reached a stage where I got as much pleasure from fielding as from batting and if I arrive for a Championship match and discover we have lost the toss, the prospect of a hard day in the field does not bother me.

It is absolutely vital to approach the job with enthusiasm. There are not a lot of rewards to be had and you have to go out and make your own satisfaction. I find that the best way to do this is by setting myself a target and starting the day intent on keeping a clean sheet. My aim is not to concede a single run, and if I can leave the field knowing no batsman pinched a single because I was dreaming, or a boundary which sneaked through my hands, then I know I have helped to serve my team.

Bowlers respond to sharp, enthusiastic fielding. They become keyed up if they know their colleagues are on their toes, anxious to prevent any runs being scored, and once the batsman is forced to take chances because the bowling and fielding is so tight, the initiative has been gained.

In the better grades of cricket, bowlers tend to bowl to their field. They place their most reliable fielders in key positions – at mid-wicket for an off-spinner for example – and attempt to bowl in such a fashion that the batsman can only hit the ball to that area.

Fielding used almost to be regarded as a necessary chore by most cricketers and it is not that long ago that teams were prepared to carry 'passengers' providing they could bat or bowl effectively. The less talented fielder was simply banished to the outfield – out of harm's way – and if he could not stop the ball with his boot when it went in his direction, no one seemed particularly bothered.

In present day cricket, however, the man who cannot play a part in stopping runs being scored is rarely selected and virtually every county now demands a high standard of fitness from its players.

At Nottinghamshire, we introduced a schedule a few years ago and I would go so far as to suggest that anyone who follows this with some degree of dedication and enthusiasm will become a better than average fielder. In fact, we adopted two schedules at Trent Bridge, the thirty minutes one which is used before the start of a day's play and the more concentrated sixty minutes one for use in practice sessions. Since these were introduced, every player on the staff has improved his fielding, if only because when the same situations crop up in a match, we have a better idea of how to handle them and react instinctively.

Here is an outline of those schedules, together with other work which I recommend should be done throughout the year. If you live in the Southern Hemisphere or the West Indies or anywhere else a long way from the UK, adjust the months accordingly.

October–December

There is a natural tendency to eat more and spend more time sitting around during these three months so it is important to work at maintaining a reasonable level of fitness. I have been fortunate in recent years because I have been away on tour. But if I stay in England, I force myself to do enough basic training to keep me in reasonable condition.

Twice a week I do long-distance runs of about six miles and along with these are shuttle runs which require sprinting and turning. In this way, you can maintain stamina and sharpness at the same time. During this period it is also useful to devise a system of circuit training, whether you have the use of a gymnasium or lacking this, have to improvise.

January–March

This is the time to begin thinking about the new season and if you have been keeping yourself reasonably fit during the previous three months, you will see the benefit of it during this period of the year.

The weather is nothing like good enough to work outside, so try to get regular use of indoor facilities where net practice will enable you to work on your timing. At the same time, practise throwing at the stumps to get your arm functioning effectively again, placing the emphasis on quickness and accuracy.

Another priority at this stage of the year is to harden your hands. This is very important because in the cold April and May days at the start of the season, split fingers are a regular occurrence if the hands have not been properly prepared. It happened to me at the start of the 1979 season when, having just returned from the tour of Australia, I wrongly assumed my hands were in the right condition. I caught a ball awkwardly in our opening Benson and Hedges match against Middlesex, needed stitches in my hand, and did not play again for a few weeks.

Initially the only way to harden your hands is by tossing a cricket ball forcefully from one to another and if this is done regularly for a few days, your work in the indoor nets will finish the job.

April

County cricketers report back in April and our normal routine at Trent Bridge is to spend the first week at a nearby sports centre where we concentrate on getting fitness back to a peak.

During the second week we devote half of the time to stamina work, with a lot of running, and the remainder to sharpening up our fielding. This is when the sixty minutes schedule comes into daily operation and we have found that the best way to maintain interest and produce high standards is by devising fielding games.

May–September

The season is now under way and providing the right amount of work has been put in during the past seven months, we are ready to meet the demands of the next twenty or so weeks.

Even though we will be playing virtually every day during this period, there is no let up where fielding practice is concerned. Every match-day morning we will go through the abbreviated version and the sixty minutes schedule is followed on days off.

The thirty minutes schedule involves five exercises, the emphasis being at all times on quality.

No 1 – This is a simple affair involving a line of players, properly spaced about 12 feet from the batsman (striker), who keeps them busy with a succession of flat catches. It is important when fielding to keep your eyes on the ball and to concentrate. A good tip is to expect every ball to come to you.

No 2 – This involves two rows of fielders who are fairly well spread out – two at the back and three in front – with the striker and wicket-keeper some 20 yards away. The idea is for the striker to clip the ball into the gaps, where it is caught or fielded and returned accurately to the wicket-keeper. We normally turn this into a game, seeing who can catch the most.

No 3 – The five fielders are stationed together about 25 yards from the striker and wicket-keeper and the ball is played along the ground into different areas. It involves sprinting to the ball, picking it up, and producing an accurate throw. This is a tough exercise because we do three of these, take a minute's rest before doing four more, and then five more after another brief rest.

I probably work harder at this than at any other exercise because it is the type of situation I often come up against in a match and it is important that I can do it to a high standard.

Two of the essentials are to attack the ball – not wait for it to come to you – and to make sure it is in your hands before you think about your next move. I often see players who are so busy thinking about a run-out possibility that they take their eye off the ball and end up fumbling it. You cannot do a thing until the ball is in your hands – then is the time to look at your target.

Once the ground fielding aspect of this exercise is complete, the same positions are maintained to

Though more commonly on duty close to the wicket, Mike Gatting demonstrates that a good player should be able to field anywhere with this perfectly judged catch on the run to dismiss Warwickshire's Gladstone Small.

practise high catches. Again, it entails a sequence of say three-four-five with a short rest period between each, the only difference being that the striker will loft the ball and the fielder must be in position under it.

No 4 – On this exercise, the striker gives the fielder a short-range catch rapidly followed by a long one in which you are either running backwards or trying to watch the ball over your shoulder. Overhead catching is exceptionally difficult and the rule is to keep your eye on the ball for as long as possible. This one-short-one-long sequence is also used for fielding and again, the quality of returns to the wicket-keeper is important.

No 5 – Slip catching is the final exercise on the thirty minutes schedule, and this entails one man throwing the ball to the striker, who edges or hits it in the direction of the ring of fielders behind him. The thrower begins by throwing underarm to simulate a spin bowler and then switches to overarm to get more speed.

The sixty minutes schedule involves three additional exercises which are aimed primarily at improving the quality of the out-fielding.

No 1 – This covers boundary fielding with the striker sending the ball a fair distance and the fielder being responsible for cutting it off and returning to the wicket-keeper. It is important to employ a second line of defence in this situation – especially on an uneven outfield – and to have the foot or body behind the ball.

No 2 – Fielding practice can be fun at times and one of the most enjoyable exercises we engage in is: throwing at one stump. Someone rolls the ball out – ten to the right, ten left and ten straight – and it becomes a competition to see who gets the most direct hits out of thirty.

No 3 – This is another exercise which invariably turns into a competition. The idea is to contrive a match situation with a batsman attempting to score two runs and becoming involved in a race against the fielder.

The wicket-keeper rolls the ball out, judging things so that it becomes a good race, and the batsman must run two before the ball is returned and the bails dislodged. We normally pick two teams with everyone going twice. It can develop into a highly entertaining contest – and, like the rest of the exercises, can do wonders for your out-fielding.

1 Fielding the ball

The ball has been stopped with both hands – the eyes watching it all the way. Now the right hand is palm forward, the left hand closing to ensure a firm grasp. The balance of the body rocks back preparatory to coming up for a right-arm throw.

2 The stop on the move

The legs bend. The left leg is forward. The right hand takes the ball, arm forward. The head is steady. The eyes watch the ball into the hand.

3 The throw

The ball is thrown in to the 'keeper on the full, with as flat a trajectory as possible, just above stump level. There is a full follow-through. The left arm swings past the left side. The right leg comes off the ground as the right side turns with the swing of the throwing arm.

4 Catching the ball

(a) Before the ball is caught. The balance of the body is forward on to both legs. Both arms are bent. Both hands are together.

(b) Coming up for the catch. The legs are straightening to come up to the height of the ball. The hands are coming together to take the catch. The eyes follow the ball as far as possible.

CLOSE FIELDING: MIKE GATTING

Mike Gatting

He was the captain at Middlesex who took over from Brearley. He knew there'd be comparisons and he was honest enough to accept that he'd never quite possess the tactical acumen or the psychological insights of his predecessor. But, in fact, he quickly proved a sound leader – by example on the field and in the dressing room. It wasn't going to be, he realised from the outset, a sinecure: there were too many strong and opinionated personalities within the county side.

Mike Gatting has guided Middlesex to success, an especially creditable achievement in the rain-ravaged summer of 1985, during which the county were often under strength because of Test calls. His optimism, one of his most obvious qualities, didn't desert him. He has a stocky, comfortable build and a jutting chin that suggest both Cockney jauntiness and a defiant, competitive nature.

He made his debut for Middlesex in 1975 and won his cap two years later. Captaincy followed in 1983. Some had thought he might end up a soccer professional like brother Steve. Mike briefly sampled teenage football with QPR and Watford – and wisely settled for cricket. The Lord's spectators liked the way he went for his shots and occasionally tut-tutted when the hook was prematurely ambitious. He was, and still is, proud of his square cut; he'd compose an innings with assertive strokes on both sides of the wicket.

In recent seasons he has matured discernibly and has responded to the demands of leadership. He was a strong candidate for the England captaincy at the time of hesitation over David Gower's appointment.

As a fielder close to the wicket, his reflexes are exceptionally sharp; he lacks nothing in courage. He has taken up most positions around the bat at some time, has acquired bruises like battle honours and has shrugged off the high-risk element with the kind of wry grin that comes from the first-class cricketers' sense of resilient black humour.

No batsman can afford to take chances when Mike Gatting is fielding close to the wicket.

(Top) Javed Miandad has edged forward in playing the ball to leg, only for Gatting to flick it back on to the stumps at lightning speed with the batsman still out of his crease. England v Pakistan at Edgbaston, 1982.
(Bottom) Gatting dives full length on to the pitch to catch out left-hander Larry Gomes inches from the ground. One of Ian Botham's eight wickets in West Indies' first innings at Lord's in 1984.

Close Fielding

You know what they say – you have to be brave or mad to field there. And I suppose there is an element of truth in that!

I speak from hard and indeed painful experience. So would Essex's Brian Hardie and many other close-to-the-wicket specialists. In exchange for the bruises, we gain a good deal of satisfaction for the catches that come our way.

Over the years, protection has increased – from just a box to a helmet, shin pads and knee guards. The fielder, whether at forward short leg, silly mid-off or silly point, deserves any legitimate protection, just as long as it doesn't impair his movement and mobility. One slightly cynical piece of advice I always pass on is this: 'You've got to stay down. If you get up, you're more likely to be hit!'

If you are a close man on the off side, you would probably limit your 'armour' to a box and shin pads. Evasive action may not always succeed but the ball would no doubt be coming low to you. On the leg side, there is more need to protect your head and upper part of your body. The ball is more likely to be in the air – perhaps the batsman is going for the sweep – and you could be in line.

But don't panic. Most close fielders are optimists by nature. They go there because their reflexes are sharp. They acquire powers of anticipation – know when to brace themselves for the catch and when to duck. Some of the catches that come their way are reflex ones. Others – and this is a lovely bonus – are dollied straight into waiting hands.

Proficient close fielders are a vital part of any side. I've been very fortunate at Middlesex. Wilf Slack has taken over from me at forward short leg and done very well indeed. Clive Radley has done an equally good job at silly mid-off. David Gower has done some splendid work for England close-in on the off side.

Most cricketers have a stint at some time at short leg. In many teams it is one of the unwritten laws for the youngest pro to go there. The experience adds to a player's insights. It indirectly increases his knowledge of batting techniques. It does wonders for his reflexes. I wouldn't like to say how much self-preservation comes into this . . .

Concentration and confidence, as in all aspects of cricket, are important. But how should you prepare yourself as the bowler approaches the wicket? It's pointless to stay down all the time – the bowler may have stopped to tie his shoelaces. I make sure the bowler is on his way and that is the moment when I get down and *watch the bat*. My task is to *anticipate* and *react*.

Yes, of course, the quality of courage does come into it. But alertness, observation (noting how the batsman is shaping up for his drive, for instance) and mobility from a standing position are just as important. I have known players who refuse to field close to the wicket. Don't persist – a fielder who lacks enthusiasm for a specific job is of no value to the side.

And here is an interesting psychological point. Some bowlers, even the most experienced ones, are on occasions affected by the responsibility of ensuring the safety of their close-in fielders. I can remember times in county cricket when my bowlers were so concerned about their silly mid-offs and short legs that their accuracy suffered.

To my mind, short leg is the hardest of the close positions. This fielder gets very little vision of the ball which comes straight to him off the bat, the pad or the glove. Such confusions are not his concern. In the case of the bat-and-pad, my advice is for you to appeal if you think it is out. It may not always be easy for the umpire but I feel he usually has the best view, looking straight down the wicket.

Let's take a look now at the slips. And when the new ball is flying and swinging around, the bowler may have as many as four slips and even a couple of gullys.

Again it's a highly specialist job. Never take the view that anyone can go into the slips or gully to make up the numbers. I am happiest of all at second slip. It's also a fact that these days more catches go to second than to first or third slip.

First slip works in close relationship with his wicket-keeper and may stand a yard behind him. There must never be any confusion of who is going for the catch flashing between the two of them. In most cases, the 'keeper will consider it his catch. The two, by practice and experience, build up the kind of understanding that avoids any uncertainty.

The second and the other slips stand, vigilant and poised, in a neat arc. The general rule is that they should be able to touch each other with arms outstretched. Second slip is probably in line with the wicket-keeper, and third slip a pace up. But, of

The perils of fielding close. Australian captain Ian Chappell lets rip with a full-blooded drive at Lord's in 1975 that has Graham Gooch running for cover. Bob Woolmer is the other fieldsman.

course, the spacing will depend on the state of play and the type of bowler.

Gully is particularly vital in one-day matches. He may have to stretch more than the slips. His is also a 'reaction-catching' position, I always consider. The ball can come to him at all heights. It may be the hard, uppish cut. Perhaps it's a flash off the back foot – or an intended drive, deceived by the bowler's swing. It can be a nice, looping catch off the gloves. But from my experience, nothing comes too easily!

This again is what you need to remember. The slip and gully positions are basically *stationary* ones. They have little time to judge the speed or the direction. Take mid-off, for example. He has the ball in his vision all the while as it approaches him. He can adjust his judgement, moving to his left or right as he comes in.

Not so the close fielder. He relies implicitly on his reflexes. There is no time to change your mind.

An element of trust comes into it, of course. If I'm fielding at short leg, the last thing I want is for the bowler to send down a half-volley on the leg stump. I've heard one or two lively exclamations from the Middlesex close fielders when, just occasionally, Phil Edmonds or John Emburey have erred in length!

Like all the other contributors in this book, I can't impress too much on you the need to practise. Watch a highly skilled and long-serving short leg like Brian Hardie. Even Brian still picks up bruises – but by seasons of experience and intuition, he has learned how to minimise the risks.

Here, in conclusion, are a few simple exercises I do in an attempt to improve my reactions:

I stand no more than 2 feet from the bat and ask a colleague to give me catches off the face of it.

I stand with my back to a thrower only 4 feet away. When he shouts 'Now', I swing round and catch the ball he has thrown either to my side or at me.

I don't devalue a tennis ball. Catching off a wall can be of real value.

I or other close fielders go in the middle of a circle, formed by team-mates. The circle is no more than 6 feet from the middle man who is kept continually in action, taking short, sharp catches which come in all directions.

Coaching Points

1 Slip fielders on the off side should watch the ball coming down the wicket on to the bat. Having settled into a crouching position, they should stay down until the ball has either been played by the batsman or gone through to the wicket-keeper. By staying 'at the ready' the fielder can more easily move up, down or sideways to take a catch.

2 The leg slips or backward short legs must watch the ball from the moment it leaves the bowler's hand to the time it reaches the batsman. They will not always see it on to the bat, but keeping an eye on the batsman's foot movements can be a guide to the direction of the ball off the bat.

3 Fielders in close-up positions on the leg side, square or in front of the wicket, should switch their eyes to the batsman just before the bowler releases the ball.

Greg Ritchie is caught by Allan Lamb off the bowling of John Emburey in the 1985 Edgbaston Test. With spinners on at each end and fielders clustered around the bat, the pressure was on the Australian batsmen who had less time to settle between balls and more balls to face per hour.

THE ALL-ROUNDER: TREVOR BAILEY

Trevor Bailey

Plodding batsmanship is not the stuff of heroes. But never has the present writer been more excited, made more chauvinistic, by the prosaic sight of two men – Willie Watson was also there with Trevor Bailey – defending their wickets. They defied the Australians all day at Lord's in 1953. The Ashes were won back. Bailey could sometimes be boring: but that day only to the unimaginative.

There was of course Brisbane, in the 1958–9 match he took seven hours and thirty-eight minutes to score 68. One can think of other examples of soporific obduracy. 'Come on, Barnacle – for Gawd's sake, get a move on.' That was the man. It wasn't that he lacked vision; there was plenty of that and sharp ideas during his years as Essex's captain and secretary. He was essentially a team man and he believed he could be of most service playing down the line or, as a bowler, giving not too much away. He was in essence a pro cricketer, the genuine thing.

Some thought he'd have been a good captain of England and he was No 2 to Len Hutton in the West Indies. Perhaps he hadn't enough bounce and bravura. But then, what about some of the others in charge? He bowled, always with heart and mind, in tandem with Bedser. It's worth remembering that he took 100 wickets nine times. He picked up some wonderful catches close to the stumps. That made him, by any standards, a fine all-rounder.

The Essex players called him 'Chief' and liked him. Those who know him best say he's a charmer and a loyal friend. In the BBC commentary box, he talks a good deal of sense with less froth than one or two of his contemporaries. Once he chased down the right wing for Cambridge and won an FA Amateur Cup medal with Walthamstow Avenue in the 1951–2 season. A picture of the triumphant team shows Bailey in hooped jersey, long white shorts down to his knees and socks round his ankles. He looks slightly overweight and more contentedly knackered than after one of his sustained midsummer bowling stints.

For a supposed slowcoach he still scored 28,642 runs (twenty-eight centuries) and took 2,082 wickets. He did the double eight times and played for his country on sixty-one occasions.

Bowling for Essex in 1950. Trevor Bailey was an outstanding fast-medium bowler with a good high action and complete command of swing and cut.
(TPS/Central Press)

Gary Sobers, the supreme example of the all-rounder: a magnificent attacking batsman with every shot in the book; a world-class bowler of left-arm fast-medium pace and of both orthodox and unorthodox (back of the hand) left-arm spin; and a brilliant fielder in any position.

The All-rounder

Nobody enjoys his cricket more than the all-rounder, because with two strings to his bow he is nearly always in the game. He has the opportunity to rectify failure, as unlike the batsman who scores nought, he can still win the match with his bowling; while, if he is unsuccessful with the ball, he can still play a match-winning innings. He is a vital ingredient for any team.

Every side needs a genuine all-rounder, preferably more than one, to provide the balance. The ideal attack for all forms of cricket, and often essential in the limited-overs game, consists of five frontline bowlers. If these five are unable to score runs, and the wicket-keeper suffers from the same weakness, the tail will be uncomfortably long. There is always a chance of three wickets falling early to the new ball, thus leaving two batsmen to provide the bulk of the score, which is asking too much. The problem would certainly be eased, possibly solved, if the team contained two or three all-rounders.

The ideal all-rounder should be worth his place both as a batsman and as a bowler. In the early stages of a cricketer's career it is easy to attain this standard of excellence, and it is not hard to achieve and maintain at senior school and club level. There is not much physical or mental strain scoring runs and taking wickets once or twice a week, just enormous fun. It starts to become difficult when the dual-purpose player finds himself in competition with expert specialist batsmen and bowlers, while he is expected to perform two jobs day after day. This is when many youngsters who have promised so much with bat and ball fail to reach the top at either.

Our First-Class County system tends to produce a large number of 'bits and pieces' players who are very valuable, especially in limited-overs cricket, where their ability to provide a lively thirty and to send down some tidy overs is much appreciated. However, their batting lacks sufficient class, and their bowling sufficient penetration, for Test matches. As a result, there is a tendency for county and international teams to prefer batsmen who can take wickets, like Graham Gooch, or bowlers who can score runs, like John Emburey, to genuine all-rounders.

Although understandably there are not many who warrant selection for their county in both departments, there are at the present time a surprising number of world-class all-rounders able to justify their place in their national side in either capacity. Imran Khan, Ian Botham, Kapil Dev, Ravi Shastri, and possibly Richard Hadlee, all fall into this very special category.

Despite the proven ability of this distinguished group to excel in both departments at the highest level, the would-be all-rounder has to realise that he must inevitably sacrifice some of his skill in both arts. If he concentrated solely on his batting he would score more runs, while he would be more successful with the ball if he concentrated purely on his bowling.

Unless he is a slow bowler, it is unlikely that he will find himself permanently occupying positions 1, 2, 3, or 4 in the order, as his bowling must to some extent take the edge off his batting. This will automatically reduce his chances, particularly in the one-day game, of playing a major innings. Conversely a five-hour century is not the ideal preparation for a lengthy spell of fast bowling.

Whenever I found myself having to bat immediately or shortly after a long stay in the field which had included plenty of overs, I found my reactions were too slow. There were also occasions after I had been involved in a protracted rearguard action with the bat, when I would take the field full of life and keen to bowl, only to discover that some of the nip had gone. Although it will be easier for an all-rounder if he is a slow, rather than fast, bowler, the life of a spinner is more tiring than is sometimes realised. It follows that, after natural ability and practice, the prime requisite for a top-class all-rounder is stamina, which has played a not inconsiderable part in the success of Ian Botham.

Having pointed out some of the snags, let us examine four advantages of becoming an all-rounder:

First, he is nearly always closely involved in the game and usually has an important, frequently vital, role to play, as Ian Botham has illustrated so often for England.

Second, it is impossible to over emphasise his value to his team. Every side needs at least one all-rounder.

Third, he can afford to be content with being less than a pure batsman or bowler. I was always delighted with fifty, whereas Len Hutton was inclined to regard anything less than a century in a county match as tantamount to failure; while again, I would be happy having taken three wickets, but Fred Trueman would want at least five.

Finally, in my opinion, there is nothing more satisfying in cricket than being an all-rounder, a view with which Gary Sobers, the greatest of them all, would undoubtedly concur.

However, those wishing to become all-rounders must remember that it is not enough to excel at just batting and bowling, as there are three departments in the game. A true all-rounder must make sure that he is also a very good fielder; indeed his aim should be to become the most accomplished in his team and here, once again, Ian Botham serves as a splendid example. Ian is not just a magnificent fielder at the highest level, but he is that dream of every captain – an *all-round fieldsman*, outstanding in any position.

There is also another type of all-rounder in addition to the one who bats, bowls and fields: the wicket-keeper/batsman. I am inclined to think his role is even more demanding. Throughout every session in the field he is the hub around which his team revolves; he can never afford to relax, having to concentrate on every ball.

Because he is likely to be involved in more dismissals than anybody, and just as a football side cannot afford a poor goalkeeper, no cricket eleven will do well with an indifferent performer behind the stumps. Although a wicket-keeper who is also a good batsman – Les Ames was probably the best example – is a considerable bonus, I would place ability as a 'keeper far above ability as a batsman. In other words, I would always pick the best wicket-keeper available rather than an all-rounder – unless of course he happened to excel at both aspects of the game.

Trevor Bailey in an unusually aggressive mood during his vital innings of 64 for England against Australia at The Oval in 1953 – the match in which England regained The Ashes after nineteen years. Gil Langley is behind the stumps.
(TPS/Central Press)

CAPTAINCY: MIKE BREARLEY

Mike Brearley

There's nothing much left to be said – or written – about captaincy. Mike Brearley appears to go down in cricketing history as the definitive authority. None would deny his qualifications. As a leader on the field he occasionally made mistakes but they were less frequent and carried more logic than those of his contemporaries. He became a sort of cult figure, especially in retrospect.

His great merit, apart from an overall grasp of the game's tactics, was an envied understanding of the human mind. It was skilfully employed in the dressing room. He knew the way to handle his men, even those within the Middlesex and England teams whose natural independence, whims and egos had to be soothed and craftily manipulated. Brearley hated all that stuff about being a scholar and, worse, a philosopher. A bit of an egghead he was; but he worked hard to make sure it didn't show too much.

As for his cricket, some said he was lucky to play for (as distinct from captaining) England and a case could be made out. Purists didn't really like that horizontally raised bat as the bowler pounded in. In fact, he could make runs with some style and was frequently at his best against belligerent fast bowling.

Here was the player who scored 4,310 runs during his four years at Cambridge and that is unlikely ever to be bettered. He was Young Cricketer of the Year in 1964 and three years later, leading the Under-25 team to Pakistan, he hit 312 not out at Peshawar. He first played for Middlesex in 1961 and was nearly thirty when he took over the captaincy in 1971. Brearley led England thirty-one times.

Gentle of voice, competitive of nature, he was known to take his time over field placings in tense one-day matches – with icy disregard for the mounting annoyance of opposing partisan spectators. Then, content at last that he had it right for Edmonds, he would walk into position himself, grey-haired, slender-shouldered, like a don impervious to the world's insensitive taunts, off to a tutorial in his own time.

Brearley the master tactician sets his field. His exceptional knowledge of the game, calmness under pressure and ability to command the loyalty of his team-mates and to lift their performance as a result, was never better demonstrated than when he led England to their remarkable victory against Australia at Headingley in 1981.

Captaincy

'Why do so many players *want* to be captain?' Derek Underwood wondered, perplexed. It is a good question. A French general was once tactlessly asked, after a famous victory, if it hadn't really been won by his second-in-command. He thought for some time before answering. 'Maybe so,' he replied. 'But one thing is certain: if the battle had been lost *I* would have lost it.'

In 1981, shortly after being recalled as England's captain, I had a letter which read curtly:

Dear Brearley,

There is an old Italian proverb: if you want to know that a fish is bad look at its head.

Yours sincerely, . . .

A captain is held responsible when things go wrong; and any rottenness in him rapidly spreads through the whole organism. Moreover, he tends to *feel* responsible when the side does badly. He may of course be right to feel responsible; but there may also have been nothing more that he could have done. You can't make a silk purse out of a sow's ear.

Captaincy can be a hassle. In club cricket, the captain has to deal with last-minute withdrawals from the team, ensure that everyone gets to the ground; and has to entertain the opposition after the match.

What is more, cricket captains do not have the luxury of being elevated above the activity of those they lead. It is easier for a football manager to 'play God', to read the riot act to the players, because he does not have to perform himself. Sales managers don't sell, foremen don't hump bricks. All cricket captains bat and field, and some bowl. We are repeatedly reminded of our own limitations as players.

Despite all this, there are, as Underwood implies, many who aspire to the job. The fact is that there are plenty of us who feel that we know best and like the idea of putting that 'knowledge' into practice. It is more agreeable to tell others what to do than to be told what to do. We like being bossy.

We also prefer stimulation to mental inactivity. There are those who, as Ranjitsinhji wrote, 'grow grey in the service of the game and are astonishingly ignorant about it'. These cricketers are content to leave tactics, man-management and the rest to others. They prefer being punted in a gondola through Venice to organising the trip and planning the route. But we actual and potential captains are a very different breed. We are struck by the length of time that may elapse between one knock and the next. Above all, we are fascinated by the complexity and variety of the game. We see that, tactically and psychologically, there is infinite scope for sense, sensitivity and flair. There are also, necessarily, almost unlimited ways in which we can go wrong.

For various reasons, the role of leadership is more significant in cricket than in any other sport. In the first place even in its shortest form each game lasts too long, and its pace is too slow for excitement to achieve all or most of a team's aims.

Then, changes in conditions and climate make an enormous difference to what is tactically required or possible. Even on one day, in one place, the ball may suddenly start to swing when the atmosphere changes, and the new ball offers totally different opportunities for attack from one fifty overs old. As a result, cricket calls for flexibility in approach by the players and, above all, by the captain. Like the conductor of an orchestra, he determines the attitude of the players and of the team as a whole to each shifting situation.

Unlike a rowing eight, a cricket team works only by dint of differentiation. The skills, like the shapes and sizes of their owners, are diverse. I have always felt it to be one of the charms of the game that it accommodates the vast Colin Milburn and the svelte Michael Holding, the towering Joel Garner and the tiny Gundappa Viswanath. Amongst the fielders, we need skilful specialists in the slips; and agile, deft movers half-way out. We need courageous close fielders; and good runners and throwers in the deep. There is the wicket-keeper, whose job is unique and calls for at least a book to do justice to its subtleties and range. A well-balanced side will have steady batsmen as well as brilliant ones; Desmond Haynes as well as Viv Richards. Indeed, Peter Roebuck, who for many years went in at No 4 for Somerset, described his job as staying in long enough to prevent Richards (the No 3) and Ian Botham (at No 5) from being at the crease together: for when they were, Botham would try to hit the ball further, and higher, than Richards, and their partnerships, though unnerving to opposition bowlers and captains, were unproductive. Roebuck's role was as vital to the team as it was unspectacular. The range in bowling skills is equally diverse, from fast to slow, with all the variations in swing, cut, bounce and spin.

The captain must know how to deploy whatever skills his players have at their disposal. He must enable them to widen their own range, to have the confidence to experiment. (My last remark, like many generalisations, is a partial truth, and the partial truth expressed by its opposite also needs saying: he must sometimes discourage experimentation in a batsman or a bowler, and insist on a dogged orthodoxy.) In short, a captain must get the best out of his team by helping them to play together without suppressing flair and uniqueness.

Even before the match begins, the captain will have to exercise his judgment. Take, for instance, wet pitches. A damp pitch makes the ball liable to move off the seam. A soaked pitch – or 'pudding' – may play easily, and the captain's advice to his batsmen may be 'get on the back foot, unless the ball is a half-volley'. As a wet pitch dries it will take spin, and then the harder it is underneath the surface the more sharply it will bounce and turn. On the other hand the ball may skim through nicely for the batsman if the pitch has merely become greasy from drizzle.

It was a great privilege for me to captain Middlesex for twelve years, and England on four tours and in thirty-one Tests, and I should like to be able to convey some of the fascination of the job at this level. But my own fascination with tactics began decades before. I have loved the game for as long as I can remember, and would, like many youngsters, persuade anyone to come and bowl to me, even as a last resort, my great-aunt. But from a very early age, my father was instilling in me not only a straight bat and a pointed left elbow (which had a suspiciously Yorkshire quality) but also a sense of who was bowling and why someone else should have been; of where certain fielders stood and why they ought to have been elsewhere (though no doubt these 'oughts' would have been misplaced during the three years that my father was himself captain of Brentham Cricket Club, in Ealing, while I grew from eight years old to eleven).

Broadly speaking the task of the captain can be divided into two areas: tactics and motivation.

Brearley the team leader gives a word of encouragement to fast bowler Graham Dilley.

Tactics involve decisions about selection and pitch, as we have seen, and it also includes the most obvious part of the captain's job – changing the bowling and placing the field. Equally important is motivation. It is no use being an expert on tactics if your team don't trust or respect you, if you are always putting people's backs up unnecessarily, or destroying their confidence. Encouragement is vitally important, not only for those who are struggling, but also for your star performers. And as you get to know your players, you will realise that some respond well to a tough line, others to softness. I found, for example, that

Botham would often bowl even better if riled, as when I teased him about his little jink before delivery, calling him the Sidestep Queen. Even so great a batsman as Geoff Boycott, on the other hand, needed to be reassured about his own batting and to hear from others that he had been unlucky in his dismissal.

Captaincy is difficult. But we must also do justice to a quite opposite idea, that it is essentially simple. A man said to me recently, 'Motivation is basically straightforward; it's a matter of bringing the best out of people.' Batsmen may be over-

Brearley the communicator has time for a television interview as he pads up for his last match before retiring, at Worcester in 1982.

coached; it is said of Ian Botham that he is a wonderfully *natural* cricketer. As Kapil Dev remarked recently, 'there is no room for *copying* anyone else's play at Test level.' Without doubt we have to be natural to be captains, too; we must be ourselves. Every good captain leads his side in his own way, as suits his own personality. He must be willing to follow his hunches. The captain, like the batsman or the mother, is impeded and stilted in his performance if his head is constantly cluttered up with theories.

The trouble is that not every spontaneous response is appropriate or valid. How can a mother 'behave naturally' if what she longs to do is strangle her brat? Or a batsman if, whenever a slow bowler tosses one up, he is irresistibly tempted to slog it over mid-wicket? It is true that captaincy is at best often a matter of intuition; but only if the intuition has been honed and trained and developed along the right lines. The heart must be in the right place, but so must the mind and its attention to detail.

The kindest, or perhaps most flattering, remark made about me as a captain was in an article by Mihir Bhose. He wrote that my 'Brahminical' attention to detail managed to avoid fussiness because the spirit of my captaincy was sound. The principle is right, though the players who played under me would by no means all, or always, have agreed with its application.

Some Advice on Aspects of Captaincy

Cricket, as has been said often enough before, is a game of infinite variety, played under conditions that vary from country to country, match to match, moment to moment. To make hard and fast rules about captaincy is therefore not only difficult, it is also rather futile since so much depends on the particular situation and the circumstances involved. Let's face it, if it could all be learnt from a book there wouldn't be such a shortage of good captains around. What follows then is more in the way of general advice than anything more categorical; something for captains and would-be captains to think about.

On winning the toss

To begin with, a lot depends on the nature of the match itself; on whether it is a limited-overs fixture or an open match, and whether there is to be one new ball or two. If there is to be only one new ball, for example, and you think you have a seam attack that can exploit it effectively, then there is a good case for putting in the opposition. You might arrive at the same conclusion, of course, if you think your own batsmen would fare badly against *their* seam bowlers. In limited-overs cricket many sides prefer to chase a target than to set one and will automatically choose to bat last if they win the toss, whatever the conditions.

Other reasons for putting in the other side are if the pitch is grassy or damp, which can help the pace bowlers, or if it looks as though the pitch will get progressively easier as the day goes on. If the pitch is hard and firm, or a real 'pudding', then you are almost certainly better off batting.

It is also important to keep an eye on the weather. If rain is likely later in the day there is some advantage to be gained from going in first and getting runs on the board. On the other hand, if it is humid and overcast and you have a bowler who can swing the ball in these conditions, it could be worth having a crack at the opposition straight away.

Setting the field

Basic settings should be worked out with all your bowlers before you take the field. These should include both attacking and defensive fields, with appropriate variations for left- and right-handed batsmen, especially when they are at the wicket together. Adjustments can then be made to meet the individual strengths and weaknesses of the batsmen, and to try and dictate the pattern of play.

It is also a sensible idea to plan in advance where to place your best fieldsmen, and where to position any 'passengers', and to make sure that your main bowlers don't have to travel too far between overs. Unless a captain is a specialist close to the wicket, like Brian Close or David Gower, the best fielding position for him is probably mid-off where he is almost in line with the wickets and can see clearly what is going on. If he happens to be a good slip fielder, he can stand at first slip where he will have a similar vantage point.

Incidentally, it can save a lot of hand-clapping and arm-waving, not to say time, if fielders can be persuaded to keep an eye on their captain for fresh instructions.

Arranging the batting order

Unless you are forced to make changes because of injury or the tactical situation, it is better not to interfere too much with the batting order once it is established. Most batsmen prefer to go in at a certain position and chopping and changing can be unsettling for them.

It makes sense to have opening batsmen who complement one another – one attacking, the other defensive in character – like Boycott and Barber in the sixties, or Gooch and Robinson today. Mixing right- and left-handers down the order is also a good tactic as most bowlers find this disconcerting; always assuming you have the batting talent at your disposal.

Team talks

Having informal team talks (that is talking *with* not *down to* your colleagues) and getting everyone thinking about the game is a good thing to do. Not only does the captain get a valuable feedback of ideas, but it boosts the morale of individual players and helps to motivate the team as a whole. Besides, talking shop is part of the fun of the game – so too, these days, is watching together videos of some of the top players in action. You can learn a lot about different skills and tactics from these films, which helps to raise the performance of the team.

Most of all, it's important that the captain enjoys his cricket and communicates that enjoyment to his team-mates. In the end the buck must always stop with the 'man in charge', but if he has a good dialogue going with his team and can command their enthusiastic support, it certainly lightens the load.

THE PSYCHOLOGICAL APPROACH: RICHIE BENAUD

Richie Benaud

When we think of Richie Benaud, the adjectives tumble from our thoughts: he was crafty, foxy, astute, mischievous. Their sum total made him a fine cricketer and a great captain. He had the acceptably mean, competitive streak that you'd expect from a top-flight Aussie. But his cricket was always undeniably attractive. He challenged the opposition to play it his way – and to search, where possible, for a result.

Richie Benaud had the supple wrists and fingers of a fine leg-spinner. He had the strength and the courage of the batsman who liked to attack. Most of all, he had the mind of the comprehensive cricketer. As long as the match went on, he was mentally ticking over. He ruthlessly played at an opponent's weaknesses; he cajoled and he kidded.

He played for New South Wales from 1948 and went on automatically to become captain. His first Test match, at the age of twenty-one, came against the West Indians in 1951–2. When Ian Craig fell ill, Benaud took over as captain of his country, in 1958. His leadership qualities soon became outstanding. He was assertively in charge in four successive series that ended in triumph for Australia.

In sixty-three Tests, he took 248 wickets. Much of his success came on hard wickets where his nagging length and subtle variation flummoxed the most proficient of international batsmen. Everyone seems to remember his farewell at Old Trafford in 1961. It was both triumphant and sentimental. He finished with 6–70 and in effect he'd saved the Ashes.

But, of course, he was in every sense an all-rounder. The broadish shoulders brought him nearly 12,000 first-class runs and twenty-three hundreds. As a fielder he was surprisingly agile for a big man and held on to many difficult catches close to the wicket. His intelligence and wisdom as a player are still savoured by the rest of us – from his perceptive observations as a writer and commentator.

Richie Benaud ranks among the great Test captains – an astute and aggressive leader who was never afraid to take risks and rarely missed a chance of putting pressure on the opposition. An outstanding all-rounder, he led by example and was the first player to score 2,000 runs and take 200 wickets in Test cricket. Seen here in action on the 1956 Australian Tour of England.
(TPS/Central Press)

112

The Psychological Approach

There is some significance in the fact that one of the greatest golfers the world has seen, Peter Thomson, has always declined to write either a book on the golf swing or one on the psychology of the game.

When the golf classic, *The Best of Longhurst*, was published it contained a three-page piece on these matters, put together by Henry Longhurst after a conversation with Thomson at a hotel overlooking St Andrews. Thomson later told me he thought he may have been a little garrulous and would have preferred to cut it to two pages.

I feel slightly like that when confronted by the task of writing about cricket thinking and adding to it the psychological approach. The psychological approach to anything in cricket is not worth a tinker's whatsit unless accompanied by at least four special ingredients. The first is luck, the other three are common-sense, a sound knowledge of gambling and an even sounder one of people.

Show me a man listed as a potentially brilliant captain and if he lacks even one of those latter three attributes, then I'll show you a potential failure. There are no half measures about luck. If it's not with you then you might as well forg· t about the psychology of being a hero.

One of the beauties of this game is that no two people are the same, nor do they bat, bowl or field in the same way. Hence the need to be a good judge of people or players; every one of them must have a slightly different approach so far as the captain is concerned.

Captains like Ian Chappell, Ray Illingworth and Mike Brearley at Test level and Keith Miller at first-class level were the best I have seen at this aspect of leadership. There were other thinking cricketers around in those eras as well, but those were the best captains I ever watched or played under. Each of them led good teams, they were lucky, they had common sense, they were certainly gamblers – even Illingworth whose exterior might have given a more dour but erroneous impression. He and the others knew when to gamble, which is even more important than merely being prepared to gamble.

Common sense means different things to different cricketers. From the pavilion I might have watched one of my batsmen get himself out at a time when I knew we needed some consolidation.

When he came back to the dressing-room he probably had a very good reason for trying to play the shot. The fact that it was unsuccessful may well have been a lack of skill rather than a lack of common sense.

Some cricketers will never play for England or Australia. That in itself will in many cases be because of a lack of skill, or even a lack of chance although the skill is there. It may be that a player is worth a Test place but his type of batting or bowling is already being produced for the team by another player who is being very successful.

There may then be a lack of opportunity, but not of common sense.

If there were to be one thing to drum into a young cricketer it would to my mind be a willingness to keep two overs ahead of the play and be prepared to back your hunches; to gamble.

The captain and the player who is only up with the play, to the extent of concentrating on the ball just bowled, will always be very solid and comforting to a county committee, a State Association or even to a Test selection panel. The one who is looking ahead when things aren't going too well and even when they are, is the one who will be winning more than he loses.

Providing his luck holds.

In 1985, in the course of some very wet Test match days, the BBC showed film of the Manchester Test of 1961. This match had special significance for me because it saved my neck. As it also happened in the series following the one where Jim Laker bowled so magnificently against us, Old Trafford could hardly have been regarded at that stage as one of Australia's happiest cricket grounds.

This was the first time I had seen the full film of that England second innings and there was definitely a degree of luck. Ted Dexter got an outside edge to a top-spinner, Raman Subba Row was bowled off his pads just before tea and John Murray and David Allen were caught at slip by Bob Simpson, two of the finest reflex catches of their kind you will ever see in any class of cricket.

Common sense came into it as well.

When the decision was made and transmitted to the rest of the players that we had to change tactics and bowl England out, it was for a very good reason. The other option – getting out of it with a draw – had been blotted out in the glory of Ted Dexter's· strokeplay. Now it was a case of being prepared to gamble and knowing when to gamble; it was also a matter of knowing your team.

The only other thing I asked was that they should gear themselves for the greatest fielding exhibition of their lives, which they proceeded to do.

There have been other matches with a denouement of that kind, sometimes not working out the way one might wish, but certainly covering the four aspects of captaincy mentioned above . . . plus the ever-present requirement of keeping two overs ahead of the play.

The psychology of cricket seems more and more to be given an airing these days. We have cricketing seminars and players who have been given what is termed a 'psychological boost' to ready them for the task ahead. All this is well and good, providing you don't get too carried away with it.

For example, a psychological boost can never take the place of good old-fashioned skill and a decent helping of courage. If you don't have the skill, a thousand seminars will not give it to you; if you waver momentarily when the pressure is on, you will not be saved by someone at a seminar shouting and waving a fist in your face. What matters is that you must *want* to play and to fight and to win, that you *want* to be there when the going is at its toughest.

England beat Pakistan at Headingley in 1982 because they kept cool heads when Pakistan did not and because Pakistan could not bring themselves to gamble when the crunch moment came. Australia in the end beat England at Lord's in 1985 because Border, when that crunch moment appeared, took the gamble and instructed O'Donnell, the least experienced player in the team, to hit the slow bowler down the ground.

Kenny Rogers has it right in that delightful ballad 'The Gambler' when he sings of the cards held by the greatest poker players:

> You've got to know when to hold 'em,
> Know when to fold 'em,
> Know when to walk away,
> And know when to run . . .

I suppose there is a threat of psychology there – I must ask Peter Thomson when next I see him. Perhaps we could make him happy and reduce his three pages to four lines.

Applying the wrong kind of psychological pressure. Dilip Vengsarkar complains about Phil Edmonds talking to him while fielding at short leg. Umpire David Evans and Indian captain Sunil Gavaskar go to investigate, while Chris Tavaré, Ian Botham and Derek Pringle in the slips await the outcome. England v India at Lord's, 1982.

GETTING EQUIPPED: ALF GOVER

Alf Gover

He once took four wickets with consecutive balls, just as fellow Surrey players Alan Peach and Pat Pocock did. His feat, at Worcester in 1935, rightly earned him the mounted cricket ball and much congratulation at the time. But it appears he was never averse to such a streak of theatricality. In 1946, the summer he made the last of his four Test appearances, he was fielding at short leg for Surrey against Combined Services. Team-mates are insistent that he was lifting his sweater in a gesture of self-protection and could see nothing. Incredibly, the ball lodged between his legs. Jim Laker had no complaints about such unorthodox close-fielding methods – they brought him his first wicket for the county.

Alf Gover took 1,555 wickets and he didn't always have too much luck himself. The first time he played for England, against India at Manchester in 1936, two catches were dropped off his bowling and he ended the match with nothing to show from the two innings.

He was a well built, wholehearted fast bowler with a rather ungainly action and initially with a problem over his run-up. Opposing batsmen feared his outswinger and a break-back that at times was virtually unplayable. He was an intelligent and canny operator with the new ball, and his compounded knowledge and wisdom – as it affected the batsman as well as the bowler – have benefited successive generations of young cricketers at his famous indoor school.

A great many top-class players also have reason to be grateful for his considerable skills as a coach. International stars, like Viv Richards and Andy Roberts, Colin Cowdrey and Frank Tyson, are quick to nominate him among the valued influences in their exceptional progress. For years, his lucid and practical advice, contained in his coaching column for *The Cricketer*, has guided and 'straightened-out' young players; likewise his series on television.

Gover was born in Surrey but flirted briefly with Essex, with whom ironically he travelled as twelfth man to The Oval, before joining his native county at the bidding of Herbert Strudwick. He made his Surrey debut in 1928 and played 336 matches for them in a span, interrupted by the war, until 1947. There would have been greater Test recognition but for the contemporary presence of Larwood, Voce, Gubby Allen, Bowes, Farnes and Nichols. Competition could be demoralisingly keen, even for a fine bowler like Gover who twice took 200 wickets in a season.

Former Surrey and England fast bowler, Alf Gover. Note the full follow-through, an example he has passed on to generations of young cricketers as England's premier coach.
(Alf Gover)

Head right over the ball, the twenty-two-year-old Sunil Gavaskar concentrates on his defensive technique under the watchful eye of Alf Gover, at the latter's famous cricket school in London.
(TPS/Central Press)

117

Getting Equipped

It takes more than good equipment to make a good player, but having the right equipment and maintaining it properly can certainly improve your performance.

For the majority of cricketers choosing a bat is the main job at the beginning of a new season. Many come into our shop at the Cricket School airing their knowledge about wide or narrow grain, though the width is relatively unimportant. The grain of a bat is peculiar to the tree the wood has come from, and often to the actual part of the country itself where the tree has grown. The important thing to look for is that the width of the grain is consistent, that it is in a straight line and does not lose its line on any part of the blade. The best width to have is between six and fourteen grains and the harder you hit the ball, or the earlier that you are in the batting order, the narrower the grain should be because the bat is harder.

The fellow who is a big hitter should always look for a heavy bat (upwards of 2lb 8oz) and for added insurance preferably one with a protective covering. The modern type of protection adds nothing to the weight and is barely visible. The stroke-player should look for a lighter blade.

There is a tendency these days for some young players to try and copy the likes of Ian Botham and Graham Gooch by choosing a heavy bat, only to find that it is too much for them to handle. Having a heavy bat is no guarantee of being able to hit the ball harder. The aim should be to select a bat that feels comfortable and suits your style of play, one that you can wield effectively through all the strokes.

The width of handle should be taken into consideration depending on the size of the player's hands. Those with big hands often prefer an extra grip. A short-handle bat is usually recommended for players 5ft 11in and under, and a long handle for taller players. However, a shorter player with a very upright stance may prefer a long handle. It is wrong to use a handle which makes you tip over so much that you cannot play your shots and be balanced.

Having chosen your bat, you should look after it properly so that it gives you good service. The covered bat will not of course require oiling, and care should be taken not to over oil those bats that do. Many players are under the mistaken impres-

sion that oiling improves the performance of the bat; oiling is simply to stop the bat drying out and to keep the wet out. Viewed through a high-speed camera it can be seen that both bat and ball give a little on impact; oiling helps to prevent the willow getting dry or damp and splitting as a result. Over oiling will make the face of the bat too soft; it is important not to use the bat until the oil has been well and truly absorbed into the willow.

Particular care must be taken playing the bat in. Using a bat mallet or a ball in a sock, lightly tap the face and sides of the bat all over for about ten minutes each day for three to five days, so that the effect is the same as playing with it but in a highly controlled way. It is best then to try your new bat out in the nets; and when you are there make sure the bowlers are using old balls that will be soft with the seams flattened. A new ball, hard and with a prominent seam, may soon crack the surface of a new 'toy'.

During the season when the bat requires cleaning, or about every six weeks, a light rub with sandpaper and then a wipe down with an oily rag will bring it back to normal. During a wet spell the toe of the bat should be dried off, or left overnight standing on toilet paper, otherwise the dampness will result in the toe swelling and the bottom splitting. Then re-oil the toe.

Left-handed players should never use bats made for right-handed players as this could cause unnecessary damage to the bat. Never continue playing with a damaged bat.

Pads should be strong and well padded both inside and out; lightweight pads give greater mobility but make sure that they give good protection as well. The straps and buckles should be sewn through at least two seams. With your leg bent your knee should fit into the centre of the knee roll. To service pads use a top quality whitening; this not only smartens them up, but also gives them a longer life. Do this to buck and canvas pads; plastic pads only require a wipe down with a cloth which has been dipped in a mixture of water and washing-up liquid.

Batting gloves should fit snugly and have strong, firm padded protection covering not only fingers and knuckles but also the back of the top hand. Remember that gloves must give protection and the padding may be a little stiff at first; the heat of your hand will soon mould them. Many gloves are now pre-curved for more immediate comfort. Thin cotton batting inners will soak up the sweat and thereby preserve your batting gloves. But gloves and inners must be dried out naturally before being put away.

Wicket-keepers' gloves should also fit snugly with the finger tips to the end of the gloves. The padding on the palms must be pliable, never so that it restricts the cupping. The cuffs, even on the modern mitt type, should protect the wrist. Gloves should be moulded to the natural cupping shape of your hands by constantly closing the fingers to the palm and by throwing a ball from hand to hand. Inner gloves can be chamois or cotton; thicker inners give more protection but of course less feel. Chamois inners need only to be moistened, not soaked, by flicking a fine spray of water on to them – that's all. Dry both gloves and inners naturally by putting them over a coat hook; never put them away damp. Gloves should always be re-faced at the end of each season.

Footwear is sometimes neglected by club players. All bowlers should wear spiked boots; fast bowlers will need stronger boots with higher ankles and thicker cushioned heels for support, whilst slow bowlers can have lower cut shoes. Rubber studded soled boots are recommended for batsmen and fielders in dry conditions. Smooth soles are no good at all, and shoes with soft toes can be dangerous – a ball landing on your foot can put you painfully out for the rest of the game, if not for several games. Boots should be examined after each game to check if any studs are missing or have become loose.

Always, always wear a box (abdominal protector) when batting, wicket-keeping or fielding close to the bat. The padded type is best and we recommend that youngsters from the age of nine should wear one.

There are now several types of trousers on the market, and which style you go for is largely a matter of taste. Batting trousers are now made more for comfort than appearance, using slightly stretch non-creasing materials. The only disadvantage of these modern stretch cloths is that they can make you rather hot on a sunny day. Grass stains are always a problem to remove, but we have found that by first giving the stained part of the trousers a good soaking in strong detergent water, then dry cleaning them, this can do the trick. Another method is to soak the stain in Biotex and then wash or dry clean.

Shirts are made long-sleeved or short-sleeved in poly-cotton which has slight stretch, or in cotton which soaks up the sweat more but needs ironing. We always recommend a half-size bigger than normal to allow greater freedom of movement.

Acrylic sweaters and slipovers are cheaper but not as warm as wool which is more expensive and needs more care. Woollen garments should be gently hand-washed, then placed in a pillow slip – the ends fastened with safety pins – before being put into a washing-machine to spin dry. When they are taken out of the machine, don't hang them up but lay them flat; this will prevent the material stretching.

Helmets are being worn by quite a few club cricketers these days, though, strictly speaking, someone playing at that level only needs a helmet if he is batting on a bad pitch where the ball can behave unpredictably. On good pitches it shouldn't be necessary to wear one as the batsman is unlikely to be facing genuine pace. Having said that, some players just feel safer, whatever the circumstances, if they are sporting a helmet, which is fair enough. They can take a bit of getting used to and it is obviously important to have one that doesn't restrict your vision or movement.

As for wearing a helmet when you are fielding close to the wicket at club level – well, if you are standing so close that you need a helmet, then perhaps you shouldn't be fielding there at all. There are easier ways of committing suicide!

KEEPING FIT AND INJURY FREE: BERNARD THOMAS

Bernard Thomas

For seventeen tours, until he chose recently to retire, Bernard Thomas eased England's aches and pains. He was the Test team physiotherapist, a small, canny, efficient man who always accepted that the job involved far more than pulling out the smelling salts or massaging a strained thigh. He was an amiable drill instructor ('Up 2–3–4 . . .' was the catchphrase he lived with), a confidant about matters medical and occasionally personal, and the chap who discreetly checked on the food in a few suspect foreign hotels.

Bernard started for England when he went out with Colin Cowdrey's side to Pakistan in 1969, five years after he began looking after the creaking joints in the Warwickshire dressing room. He stayed in charge till after The Oval Test in 1985. Then he went back to devote his full time to the sophisticated clinics that he runs in the Midlands.

Television viewers would see him dart onto the pitch with his spray and his soothing words. He was a neat, bespectacled figure who seemed to come only up to Bob Willis's rib-cage. His box of tricks was never far away and the range of his antidotes reassured the players, many of whom are by nature inclined to be hypochondriacs.

He never really played cricket himself. But he was a fine gymnast, an international judge and a chairman of the British Amateur Gymnastic Association. His fitness was legendary and his ageless agility shamed younger men of Test-match status. He was invariably an early bright-eyed riser on tour; it was sometimes claimed with the licence of camaraderie that he was starting his morning jog when the last of the team were heading for bed.

Bernie 'The Bolt', which in a way dates him and the former cricketers who labelled him after a character in that old Sunday afternoon crossbow show on television, had both knowledge and wisdom as a physio. Some would also put him in the life-saving class – and Ewen Chatfield, who played a ball from John Lever onto his temple in Auckland, would readily testify to that.

(Top) *Not a rehearsal of* Swan Lake *but a limbering-up session for the England team under the direction of Bernard Thomas as part of the build-up for the England v India series in 1979.*

(Left) *No laughing matter for Bob Willis as he lifts a leg for Bernard Thomas at Trent Bridge in 1979. Fellow England fast bowler Mike Hendrick thoughtfully reflects that it is his turn next.*

(Right) *Ian Botham is put through his paces on the jogging machine at Bernard Thomas's health clinic in Edgbaston before England's tour of the West Indies in 1980–1. Tour manager Alan Smith and Bernard Thomas study the results.*

Keeping Fit and Injury Free

The subject of fitness for cricket and cricket injuries is a complex one to cover within the confines of a single chapter, but, very simply, the higher your aspirations in the game, the fitter you should be to achieve them. Aim at 120 per cent fitness so that you always have a little in reserve.

Fitness can be divided into three basic components: stamina, strength and mobility. Think of fitness as an equilateral triangle, each side representing one of these factors, and all equally important.

Stamina is the ability to maintain your level of activity without tiring. It can be improved by activities such as running, skipping or cycling for periods of 10–20 minutes, ensuring that you maintain your efforts and get out of breath.

First check your pulse to establish your normal rate. You can do this by placing the forefinger on the wrist and counting the beats in one minute. The books tell us that the normal resting pulse is 72 beats per minute, but in a highly trained sportsman this can be as low as 45–50.

Then work yourself to a maximum rate of 200 less your age; for example, a healthy, fairly fit twenty-five-year-old can work to a maximum of 175 beats per minute. After exercise, check your pulse immediately and re-check after two minutes rest, by which time the pulse rate should be returning well towards your normal.

If, however, you are overweight, unfit or over forty, work to a maximum of 180 less your age (ie 135 for a forty-five-year-old). Provided you are in good general health (check with your doctor first if in doubt), these methods will give you a useful guide as to your improving fitness: you can test your progress by how soon you get out of breath and how quickly the pulse rate returns to normal.

Excessive strength or muscle bulk is not quite so essential for cricket as for many other sports, but you do, of course, require sufficient strength to deliver the ball, swing the bat and move around at speed. An ideal form of strength training is that involving your own body weight – push-ups, step-ups, etc, which can be progressed by increased repetitions or the addition of a small weight in the hands. A limited amount of weight training is helpful – strong legs will enable you not only to cover distances at speed but also to bend for the ball when you reach it! Keep your abdominal muscles strong as you are then less likely to be overweight, and your posture and co-ordination will be better controlled.

Also use the 'tools of the trade': swing your bat, and practise running in your pads.

Mobility applies to both the joints of the body and to the surrounding muscles, ligaments and tendons – the 'soft tissues'. Much apparent joint restriction is the result of tightness in the soft tissue; tight hamstrings are but one example. It is equally important to maintain full and free movement in the hips, knees, neck and shoulders – include in your training routine exercises such as wide stride sitting and bending forward from the hips; head and shoulder circling; and toe touching. Mobility is not quite so easily assessable as the other two factors in our triangle, but it is equally important as it has considerable bearing on the next section – namely, avoiding injury.

Most cricket injuries can be divided into two categories: direct and indirect injuries.

Direct injuries are those caused by an external force – a fast rising ball, an uneven pitch or even a collision between two players. Here we should give some consideration to protective equipment.

Boots

These should give your feet adequate protection; never bat in training-type shoes. Make sure that they also give you adequate support, and don't forget the simple precautions such as avoiding foot holes when marking your run-up.

Pads

Make sure they fit correctly and comfortably with no restrictions at any point. Forearm, chest and thigh protectors are useful – remember that it is not only your leading leg which may be hit whilst batting; many a painful blow has been suffered high on the inside of the rear leg.

Helmets

These should give you not only maximum protection but also optimum vision. Make sure that the visor or faceguard is correctly positioned, and always use a chinstrap – a helmet which flies off at the slightest action is a potential danger in itself.

Gloves

Match your gloves to the grip you use, as ill-fitting gloves may leave parts of the knuckles and fingers exposed to injury.

Boxes

These should be of sufficiently strong material not to crack on impact as this in itself is a potential source of injury.

Remember, too, that close fielders also require adequate protection, which may include shin-guards and knee-protectors in addition to the more obvious helmet and box. Try to avoid borrowing equipment from other players, and wear your own equipment in the nets so that it feels part of you.

Should you be unfortunate enough to sustain an impact injury, do not carry on if in doubt, particularly with a head or facial injury. Even the best qualified medical adviser cannot always identify a possible delayed concussion on the field and, of course, possible fractures in this area always require immediate attention.

An ice pack or cold spray can relieve simple bruising to enable a player to carry on when necessary, but always seek medical advice if in any doubt.

Indirect injuries are those that occur within the body, often associated with sudden movements, incorrect suppling exercises, or inadequate pre-match warm-ups. It is essential during training sessions to maintain the maximum amount of joint, ligament and muscular suppleness, but progress with care and never snatch your movements. Practise your throwing by limiting the distance at first and building up to full distance – it is here that assiduous preparation on shoulder strength and mobility will prevent the 'throwing out' of the joint so commonly seen in cricketers. Constant movement when on the field and a thorough warm-up before each match session will help you to remain prepared for sudden bursts of activity.

Here again, attention to your footwear plays an important role in injury prevention. Make sure you have adequate heels on your boots to help avoid Achilles tendon or calf strains, and take advice on your spikes according to the conditions on the field – these can vary tremendously within the space of one match.

If you are the victim of such an injury, which does not settle quickly, do seek advice. It is not worth nursing a persistent injury when prompt treatment will see a return to your enjoyment of the game in the shortest possible time.

Exercise 1

Starting position: Wide stride sitting.
Action: Reach towards the foot, taking the chest down to the thigh (not head to knee). This ensures a maximum stretch of the hamstrings and adductors, without throwing strain on the back.

Exercise 2

Starting position: Wide stride sitting
Action: Reach down to both ankles (or the nearest point), taking the chest towards the floor to obtain maximum stretching in the general area of the hips. Avoid undue flexion of the spine or strain on the back.

Exercise 3

Starting position: Wide stride hands on the floor to an approximate distance as shown.
Action: Stretch the shoulders back, keeping the arms straight, and take the head and chest towards the floor. This loosens the shoulders, lengthens the spine and loosens the adductors and hamstring muscles.

UMPIRING: DICKIE BIRD

Dickie Bird

No-one would dispute that Harold 'Dickie' Bird is the best known umpire in the world. Many would reinforce that statement by saying he's also the best. For all those oddball extrovert mannerisms and jokey asides, he always looks thoroughly in control. The players like and respect him. Just occasionally they may pull a face but, in retrospect, they accept that he is likely to be right. They don't harbour a grievance.

He comes from Barnsley, not far from where he still lives, and played for Yorkshire during 1956–9. There were only fourteen matches for his native county and he wishes passionately there had been more. In 1960–4, he was with Leicestershire but he says he never really settled at Grace Road. He was a right-handed opening bat and bowled at medium-pace. Despite the frustration as a player, he scored his 1,000 runs in 1960.

Dickie was a useful schoolboy footballer, a contemplative inside forward who made decisions and sprayed passes in his own unhurried time. He was good enough to sign for Barnsley. But there was invariably a greater appeal in opening the innings.

He became a first-class umpire in 1970 and made his Test debut three years later. Since then, he has stood in nearly 100 international matches. No other umpire has officiated in all three World Cup finals. He also stood in the women's World Cup final but not, one assumes, in pursuit of a wife. Yet in a slightly poignant confidence, he says: 'If I've missed anything because of my obsession with cricket it's marriage and family life. I regret that deep down . . . I think I'd have made a good father.'

The vowels belong to South Yorkshire; so do the attitudes. He can be blunt as well as warm. He has a gregarious side, is a popular top-table guest and draws an audience whenever he goes into one of his good-humoured monologues. His favourite ground is Lord's – 'because of its atmosphere, tradition and mystique, I suppose'. Chesterfield and Tunbridge Wells don't come far behind. And it doesn't seem as though there are any honours left for him to pick up.

A controversial dismissal in Australia's second innings against England at Edgbaston in 1985. (Top) Wayne Phillips square cuts a ball from Edmonds, which hits the leg of Allan Lamb as he tries to take evasive action.
(Middle) David Gower turns towards the ball as it shoots up into the air off Lamb's leg.
(Bottom) Having caught the ball, Gower and the other England players appeal. Umpire Shepherd at the bowler's end was unsighted and had to confer with Umpire Constant before giving Phillips out. Australian captain Allan Border later lodged a complaint about the decision.

Umpiring

I've been lucky enough to achieve every known honour in the umpiring world and my long list of internationals, approaching a hundred as I write these words, includes three World Cup finals.

So it's reasonable for you to ask me – and me to ask myself sometimes – what makes a successful umpire? What are the necessary qualities?

It's easy enough to trot out the obvious ones. I am thinking of application, dedication, concentration and complete impartiality. But to me there is another essential – and I'm inclined to put it right at the top – the absolute need to gain and keep the respect of the players. I like to think I have this throughout the world and this is of tremendous value.

Television viewers are apt to see me talking or joking with the players during a match. I may have the occasional drink with them afterwards. This kind of relationship is healthy but I have certain self-imposed rules. I don't start chatting to players unless they speak to me first; and I never, never enter into controversies.

I can't stress too strongly how unwise it is for an umpire to allow himself to be drawn into an issue about a decision made during the match. He must not become involved. His job is to remain detached. Banter good-naturedly with the players by all means – but discreetly walk away if someone tries to broach the subject of a marginal run-out or leg-before.

Just now I catalogued some of the qualities I felt an umpire needed. I think I should extend the list. Certainly a sense of humour helps. So does the ability to remain calm and unflappable under pressure. So does the advantage of having a skin like an elephant!

The umpire must be able to live with his decisions. If he starts to worry and becomes almost neurotic, then his judgment is going to suffer.

He's bound to make mistakes. We do in every walk of life. That's part of human nature. But the unfortunate umpire must learn to cast the memory of that fleeting misjudgment immediately out of his mind. The most important thing for him is THE NEXT BALL.

Some decisions are easier than others, of course. Bat-and-pad catches can often be tricky. To me, the close run-out is the most difficult of all. And that brings me to the other umpire.

Umpires work together, in pairs. They are personal friends and it is part of their job to help each other. If the umpire at the bowler's end is uncertain about a low catch, there is absolutely nothing wrong with him going across to consult the umpire at square leg, who is probably in a better position to know what happened.

In all cases, as you will know, the advantage must be given to the batsman if the umpire is anything less than 100 per cent certain. *If a batsman is given out, there must never be any doubt at all in the umpire's mind.*

There are always murmurs of so-called cheating

To play or not to play? That is the question confronting Umpires Dickie Bird and David Constant during the Centenary Test at Lord's in 1980. Ten hours of play were lost through rain, and in a shameful incident on the Saturday afternoon Umpire Constant was assaulted by a group of MCC members angry at there being no cricket.

Umpire David Constant is perfectly positioned to judge Nottinghamshire's Chris Broad run out in the 1985 Nat-West Final.

– about that batsman or that wicket-keeper. Such innuendoes don't wash with me. I have umpired at all levels, against all countries, at times in matches which involved some of the world's most controversial figures, and I have never found them anything but fair and honest.

All right, so some of them don't walk. They wait for me to make the decision. There is nothing in the laws of the game which say they must walk. It's their right to stay their ground.

As a player with Yorkshire and Leicestershire, I always walked myself. And yes, of course it does make the umpire's job that much easier when the batsman takes it upon himself to head back for the pavilion without looking up for the umpire's judgment. But he doesn't have to – he's doing nothing illegal or under-handed.

An umpire needs to be fit. The intense mental concentration is bad enough but he's also on his feet, fielding if you like, for the *whole* of the match. No chance for him to put his feet up, like the wicket-keeper or the batsman after he's out. It's a long working day, often (no, not in 1985) in the blistering sun.

I don't smoke, drink very moderately and am always in bed by half past ten. Every morning I do 20 minutes of general exercises in my bedroom. Before each season, I do short 12–15 yard sprints; they can be very useful, especially in relation to run-out decisions and during the one-day matches when everything is so hectic.

Umpiring is tiring. So the challenge to remain as mentally alert and sharp as ever is that much greater. I'm apt to talk to myself in mid-afternoon when my concentration could so easily relax. 'Come on, come on!' I tell myself. 'Keep concentrating!' It always works. I wouldn't be surprised if you've seen me talking to myself. I don't know what the players think sometimes . . .

That brings me to my mannerisms, I suppose. People see them on the telly and puzzled Test match commentators have been known to go into lengthy discussions. The explanation is very simple. I'm a highly-strung individual. My mannerisms help me to unwind. Quite often, I promise you, I don't even know I'm doing them.

Has it helped me to have been a county player myself? Yes, of course it has. I have found it a tremendous advantage – I see things that I have gone through myself. However let me quickly point out that it doesn't automatically mean the ex-first class player makes the *best* umpire.

The umpire carries various pieces of basic equipment in his pocket. There are the obvious 'spares' – balls, bail and so on. He carries a rag, his counters for checking off the deliveries (I use miniature beer barrels), knife and Elastoplast.

Experience has taught me also to take out with me chewing gum, needle and cotton and scissors. Players are always asking me for a stick of chewing gum and in the course of a season it costs me a fortune. The needle and cotton are needed occasionally for some improvised stitching or torn flannels.

And the scissors? You'd be surprised. In one of

the Test matches with India in 1974, Sunil Gavaskar asked me to come to his aid – he wanted me to cut his hair, so that it wouldn't go in his eyes during an innings!

As I went to some pains to point out in my book, *That's Out*, I think it would be a sad day if electronic aids were introduced to complement the powers of the umpires. I frankly just can't see how such aids would help with lbw decisions or, for instance, bat-and-pad catches. In the case of the lbws there are so many things to consider, like the movement of the ball off the seam or through the air. Electronics might help with the close run-out but that is virtually all.

Now I come to the thorny topic of 'bad light'. Nothing appears to cause more controversy or in some cases bad feeling than the spectacle of players coming off the field because of poor light. I've got some sympathy with the spectators. They've paid to see a day's cricket and it frustrates them when the match is held up.

I think it calls for a one-season experiment. Try to play *in all light*, even if it means that fast bowlers like Malcolm Marshall are still bowling.

There would need to be safeguards. I'd like to see a clause that when the light has deteriorated, the ball *must* be pitched up to the bat. If not, then call No Ball and perhaps withdraw the bowler.

I accept that not everybody would agree. That's why I say we should give it a try for *one* season.

Dennis Amiss dives for the crease as Wasim Bari whips off the bails. The umpire has just a split second in which to take in the action, and to make a decision. In this case, Umpire Bird found in favour of the batsman, who went on to score 183. Dickie Bird later wrote that on seeing the television replay he thought that Amiss may well have been out. England v Pakistan at The Oval, 1974.

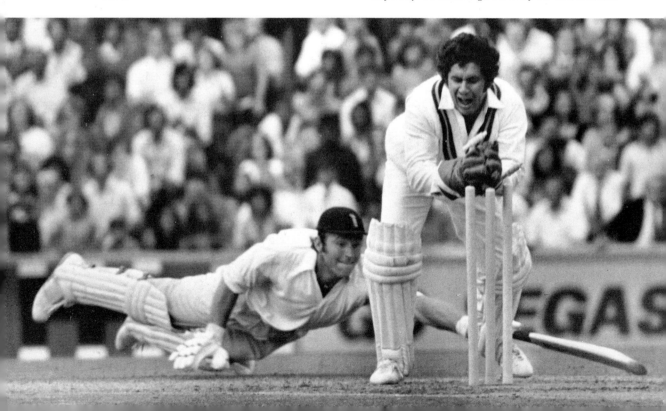